STEVEN MOFFAT

Steven Moffat was lead writer and executive producer of BBC One's *Doctor Who* from 2009 to 2017, and the co-creator, writer and executive producer of the BBC series *Sherlock* and the BBC/Netflix series *Dracula*.

His earlier work included all forty-three episodes of the teen drama series *Press Gang*, and the sitcoms *Coupling*, *Chalk* and *Joking Apart*.

Other credits include the TV adaptation of *The Time Traveler's Wife* for HBO and Sky Atlantic, an original four-part series *Inside Man* for BBC/Netflix, the TV series *Jekyll* and feature film *Tintin*.

His numerous awards include BAFTAs for *Press Gang* and *Doctor Who*, two BAFTAs and two Emmys for *Sherlock*, and the BAFTA Special Award in 2012. In 2015 he was created an OBE for services to drama.

Steven Moffat

THE
UNFRIEND

NICK HERN BOOKS
London
www.nickhernbooks.co.uk

A Nick Hern Book

The Unfriend first published in Great Britain as a paperback original in 2022 by Nick Hern Books Limited, The Glasshouse, 49a Goldhawk Road, London W12 8QP

The Unfriend copyright © 2022 Steven Moffat

Steven Moffat has asserted his right to be identified as the author of this work

Cover design by Bob King Creative for Chichester Festival Theatre, photograph by Seamus Ryan of (left to right) Amanda Abbington, Reece Shearsmith and Frances Barber

Designed and typeset by Nick Hern Books, London
Printed in Great Britain by Mimeo Ltd, Huntingdon, Cambridgeshire PE29 6XX

A CIP catalogue record for this book is available from the British Library

ISBN 978 1 84842 964 2

The Unfriend was first performed at the Minerva Theatre, Chichester, on 21 May 2022, with the following cast (in order of appearance):

ELSA	Frances Barber
PETER	Reece Shearsmith
DEBBIE	Amanda Abbington
ALEX	Gabriel Howell
THE NEIGHBOUR	Michael Simkins
ROSIE	Maddie Holliday
PC JUNKIN	Marcus Onilude

Director	Mark Gatiss
Designer	Robert Jones
Lighting Designer	Mark Henderson
Sound Designer	Ella Wahlström
Video Designer	Andrzej Goulding
Casting Director	Charlotte Sutton CDG
Voice and Dialect Coach	Charmian Hoare
Associate Designer	Ben Davies
Associate Video Designer	Adrien Corcilius
Assistant Director	Gavin Joseph
Production Manager	Kate West
Costume Supervisor	Binnie Bowerman
Props Supervisor	Lisa Buckley
Company Stage Manager	Michael Dennis
Deputy Stage Manager	Imogen Firth
Assistant Stage Manager	David Purdie-Smith

Characters

PETER
ELSA
DEBBIE
ALEX
THE NEIGHBOUR
ROSIE
PC JUNKIN

This text went to press before the end of rehearsals and so may differ slightly from the play as performed.

ACT ONE

Deck of Cruise Ship

Simply indicated – a row of deck chairs at the front of the stage.

Above this – and at all times – there is a screen that shows additional action. At the moment it shows the sky and the sea.

PETER *and* ELSA, *sitting on deck.* PETER (*mid-forties*) *is studying his laptop with a frown.*

Two deckchairs along, is ELSA *– they are clearly acquainted with each other, but are not fellow travellers. She is a powerful battleaxe of a woman, hard to guess her age.*

When they speak she is obviously American – drawling, confident, unabashed – and he is English – mordant and always slightly cross.

ELSA. What are you looking at?

PETER. Donald Trump.

ELSA. Why?

PETER. He makes me angry.

ELSA. Do you like being angry?

PETER. I love being angry. I never know what I think about anything until I'm against it. It's why I read the *Guardian*.

ELSA *contemplates this for a moment.*

ELSA.…I don't have a relationship with anger.

PETER. A what, sorry?

ELSA. I'm never really angry about anything.

PETER. How can you start the day without hating someone? It's why they have news in the morning.

ELSA. I guess I just really like people. I'm people positive.

PETER. Yeah?

ELSA. It's just who I am. I don't hate anyone.

PETER. Yeah? What about him?

He shows her the picture on his laptop. She studies it for a moment, considers.

ELSA. I'd do him.

PETER. Donald Trump??

ELSA. Yeah. I think he's funny. I'd do him.

PETER. *Look* at him.

ELSA. I'm looking.

PETER. He's ancient.

ELSA (*shrugs*). My husband's dead – the bar is low.

PETER. Don't say that. Don't you sit there and say that to me. On a cruise. When I'm on holiday. Don't say you'd do Donald Trump.

ELSA. I voted for him.

PETER. No. Don't. Don't say that.

ELSA. *Everybody* voted for him.

PETER. He lost the election.

ELSA. He only lost because of fraud and people voting against him.

PETER. Voting against him is not fraud.

ELSA. Oh, Peter, you're all tense now.

PETER. I'm not tense.

ELSA. I can hear you *clenching*.

PETER. I'm not clenching.

ELSA. Oh, honey, look at you – you could snap a proctologist off at the knuckle.

PETER. I'm fine!

ELSA. Are you angry now, Peter?

PETER. Yes! Yes, I am.

ELSA. You're welcome. Enjoy!

PETER *laughs. Fair point.*

PETER. You know. I'm going to miss our deckchair chats!

ELSA. Me too. I'm always hoping you'll be here when I come out.

PETER. Likewise.

ELSA. You or somebody.

DEBBIE *enters. Also mid-forties,* PETER*'s wife – teasing, sunny.*

DEBBIE. Have you started packing?

PETER. Broadly.

DEBBIE. Hello, Elsa.

ELSA. Debbie, my sweet. Your husband is angry.

DEBBIE (*checking the laptop*). Donald Trump?

PETER. Have you seen this? Have you seen what he's done now?

DEBBIE. What's he done?

PETER. I'm still reading.

DEBBIE. Why do you have to read about Donald Trump every morning?

PETER. You won't let me have coffee.

DEBBIE. Your *doctor* won't let you have coffee, it's bad for your blood pressure.

PETER. Actually, it's irrelevant. My blood pressure finds a way.

ELSA. My husband loved coffee. He used to say 'Give me coffee or give me death!' Now he's got death. So I guess that worked out.

DEBBIE. You see? Don't you want me to be remembering you fondly some day?

PETER. It's not something I'm actively looking forward to, no.

DEBBIE. Just me then.

PETER. Oh, you're funny. Isn't she funny, my wife?

DEBBIE. So, darling – *have* you started packing?

PETER. I'm homing in.

DEBBIE. Which means?

PETER. Everything's in the cabin. I just have to put it in the case.

DEBBIE. Docking in two hours.

PETER. I know.

DEBBIE. I know you know. And I know you think, if you leave it long enough, I'll pack for you.

(*To* ELSA.) Game of chicken basically.

PETER. Slow chicken.

DEBBIE. Marriage, as it's known.

ELSA. I love your relationship. With all your remarks.

PETER. There you are, darling. Elsa loves our remarks.

ELSA (*to* PETER). You should be more happy though.

PETER. Happiness is misinformation. It's like being an antelope. Somewhere a lion is watching you.

ELSA. Are you ever in Denver?

DEBBIE. Well, no.

ELSA. Might you ever be in Denver?

DEBBIE. Well – I suppose so, it's possible –

ELSA. When you come to Denver, I want you to look me up. Elsa Jean Krakowski.

PETER. Well, of course, we'd love to –

ELSA. Promise me – I mean it. Don't you two *dare* come to Denver without looking me up.

PETER. If we're ever in Denver, we will definitely do that.

ELSA. Elsa Jean Krakowski. Promise?

PETER. We promise!

ELSA. Cross your heart?

PETER. Cross our hearts.

ELSA. Hope to die?

PETER....okay.

ELSA. My husband used to say that. 'Hope to die.' Now he's dead. And people say God doesn't listen.

DEBBIE....Anyway. I think Peter is wanting to go and pack.

PETER. Darling, are you wanting me to go and pack?

DEBBIE. Are you getting that sense?

PETER. Twenty years of marriage – it's like telepathy, but more hostile.

DEBBIE. I'll help you.

PETER. Will you?

DEBBIE. You can't be allowed to pack a suitcase on your own – you'll only get into a fight.

ELSA. You two, go pack. I'm already packed. I'm always packed, because you never know.

DEBBIE. Your friend, Barnaby. I saw him on the upper deck, if you're looking for him.

ELSA. Oh, Barnaby. I have to apologise for Barnaby.

DEBBIE. Not at all.

ELSA. I hope he wasn't weird with you.

DEBBIE. No, no –

ELSA. He's not the man he was, I'm sorry to say. Not since his daughter.

DEBBIE. Oh, I – Sorry, I didn't – … His daughter?

ELSA. It's a long story.

PETER. Yes, well probably we should –

ELSA. *Long* story. Tragic.

DEBBIE. What happened?

ELSA. I don't know if I should be saying but just among the three of us…

(*Dips her voice, conspiratorial.*) …fat.

PETER. …Fat?

ELSA. You've no idea. Clinically obese, pardon my language. Lovely girl. Such a pretty face, if you can find it. He's got a photo in his wallet – he has to *unfold* it. Like a map.

DEBBIE. You know, I don't believe half the things you say.

ELSA. You can laugh, but it's a pain in that man's heart, believe you me. He's always had issues with disfigurement.

DEBBIE. I don't think being overweight is disfigurement.

ELSA. Try telling him that, when his mother had one eye. A one-eyed mom at the school gates. He was so embarrassed. Herding all his friends to the left. He's still not over it, even now. I tell him and tell him, 'Barnaby, she's fine with one eye. If anything it will reduce the impact of your daughter.'

DEBBIE. Stop it! You're making it up.

ELSA. Ah, Debbie, you're so sweet, but you don't know. Some people, they can't be happy. Like your husband. They think everything is a judgement. They think, 'Look at my friends, I got the wrong friends.' Barnaby, he thinks, 'My mom's got one eye, my daughter's a whale with lips – how can they do this to me?' He doesn't think, 'I got people I love, who love me back.' He thinks, 'Why don't I have better people?' And that's not because he's a bad person, I don't want you to think that about Barnaby. He's just never known how to be happy. Like you, Peter. Not since he was a tiny kid. With the bedwetting. All the bedwetting. Destroyed his childhood, the bedwetting. It haunts him to this day. It's a miracle to me he can have a holiday at sea.

DEBBIE. How long have you known him?

ELSA. Thursday.

DEBBIE.... Thursday?

ELSA. In line for the buffet. That was where you saw us, wasn't it? In line for the buffet?

DEBBIE. Um. Yeah.

ELSA. Barnaby liked you. I can always tell when he likes people. He takes a little shine, I always know.

PETER. Thursday was yesterday.

ELSA. Yesterday. Yes, in line for the buffet.

DEBBIE.... well you certainly... learn a lot about people quite quickly, don't you?

ELSA. I was telling your husband. I'm people positive. When it comes to people I don't take no for an answer.

PETER. I bet you don't.

(*Checks watch*.) Anyway. I suppose – packing.

ELSA. It's been a pleasure.

PETER. Yes, it has.

DEBBIE. Great getting to know you, Elsa.

ELSA. Elsa Jean Krakowski.

DEBBIE. Elsa Jean Krakowski.

ELSA. Denver.

PETER. I hope we didn't spoil your deckchair time.

ELSA. You made it special. Thank you for making it special.

PETER. You're welcome.

ELSA. You and everyone who sat there.

DEBBIE. Goodbye, Elsa.

ELSA. Oh, let's not say goodbye. Goodbye makes Elsa sad.
    Let's say… 'Till Denver.'

PETER.… Yes!

DEBBIE. Of course!

PETER. Till Denver!

ELSA. Till Denver, Debbie.

DEBBIE. Yes. Till Denver.

ELSA. You know what? I've gonna give you my email address.

DEBBIE. Oh, good idea.

ELSA. Then you can email me, when you're coming.

DEBBIE. Yes, of course, we'll do that.

ELSA. Hang on, I got a card somewhere… if I can find it…

PETER. I'm sure we can get your details from… you know,
    someone –

ELSA. Oh, this is so silly, I can't find it. I have a card
    specifically for giving to people. Lots of cards for lots of
    people.

    DEBBIE *has pulled out a little notebook and pen.*

DEBBIE. Don't worry, just tell me it.

ELSA. Oh, you're so lovely, thank you.

DEBBIE. So what is it?

ELSA. I can't remember. I can never remember it, that's why I specifically got the cards, in case I suddenly befriend people.

DEBBIE. Oh – well –

ELSA. Write down yours. Then I'll email you, and you'll have my address.

DEBBIE....of course, yes.

She quickly scribbles on the page, tears it out, hands it to ELSA.

ELSA. Thank you, honey!

(*Flourishes the page.*) Till Denver!

PETER. Till Denver!

DEBBIE. Till Denver!

ELSA. Or who knows – London?

Peter and Debbie's House

Composite. Kitchen, living room, entrance area. There is a back door in the kitchen leading to the back garden. A front door just off the living room. There is a door leading to the downstairs toilet just by the front door. A staircase leads up to the first floor.

At the moment: empty.

A beat: the house phone starts ringing.

Ring, ring.

Ring, ring.

From off we hear a voice – a teenage male voice – calling.

ALEX (*off*). Mum!

Ring, ring.

Mum!

Ring, ring.

Mum!

Ring, ring.

Mum!

Ring –

The phone stops ringing. Silence.

Never mind.

Silence.

More silence.

Even more silence.

Then:

Ring, ring.

Mum!

Ring, ring.

Mum!

A door bangs from upstairs.

Ring, ring.

ALEX – *a grungy teenager – comes stomping down the stairs. He is solemn, phlegmatic, and everything he says is like an announcement.*

Mum!

Ring, ring.

ALEX *has reached the foot of the stairs – right next to the phone – and calls to the kitchen (which we can see is empty).*

Mum!

Ring –

He looks at the phone. Seemingly too phlegmatic even to react. He turns and starts to head up the stairs.

Halfway up:

Ring, ring.

He stops.

Ring, ring.

Mum!

Ring, ring.

He's plodding down the stairs again.

Mum!

Ring, ring.

He now answers the phone. We hear only his replies.

Hello.

(…)

Oh. Hello, Mum.

(…)

My phone *is* on.

(…)

I didn't hear it.

(…)

Because it's at Neville's.

(…)

Charging.

(…)

Because he's got a charger.

(…)

Mine's broken.

(…)

I'm not leaving it there, I'll go and get it.

(…)

When it's charged.

(…)

He'll text me.

(…)

Oh, yeah!

Through the front door, comes PETER. *Clearly just home from work.* ALEX *glances at him.*

(…)

He just arrived.

PETER. Is that Mum?

ALEX *nods.*

Does she want to speak to me?

ALEX. She's in the car – she'll be here in a minute.

PETER. Okay.

PETER *heads off into the kitchen.*

(…)

ALEX. I'll tell him.

(…)

I will, I'll tell him.

(…)

I'll *tell him.*

He hangs up, as PETER *comes back through from the kitchen, having fetched a glass of water.*

PETER. So what's happening?

ALEX. Nothing.

PETER. What did Mum want?

ALEX. Nothing. Hang on –

He raises a finger, as if concentrating on a thought.

PETER. What is it, what's wrong?

ALEX. Nothing, hang on.

PETER. Alex –

ALEX. It's okay.

(*Lowers finger.*) I thought I was going to fart.

PETER. Alex, please –

ALEX. It's okay. I think I've stabilised.

PETER. You really, really don't have to announce these things.

ALEX. People don't like surprises.

PETER. Why not go to the bathroom?

ALEX. I don't want it to escalate.

PETER. Or step outside, or go to your room…

ALEX. Why?

PETER. It's the *living* room.

ALEX. This is part of living, Dad.

PETER. Yes, but could we keep that part to the less public areas
    of the house?

ALEX. In an ideal world. The timing is unpredictable.

PETER. Yes, okay – shall we move on?

ALEX. Also, climbing the stairs to my room could be a problem
    hydraulically –

PETER. Really, never mind.

ALEX. Anything that causes repeated dilation of the anus –

PETER. Enough, please.

ALEX. Okay.

PETER. Are you remembering about the weekend?

ALEX. Yes.

PETER. Good.

ALEX. Remembering what?

PETER. We've got someone coming to stay. Remember we told you that?

ALEX. Did you?

PETER. Yes.

ALEX. Was I listening?

PETER. Well you were physically present and facing the right way.

ALEX. Who's coming?

PETER. Just someone we met on holiday.

ALEX. Who?

PETER. Do you remember we went on that cruise, your mum and me?

ALEX. No.

PETER. We were away for a month.

ALEX. Okay.

PETER. Well we met this nice woman and she emailed. A lot. There were a *lot* of emails – really quite a lot – and in the end we just ran out of – … Well, basically, she's coming to stay.

ALEX. Why do you always have *people* here?

PETER. We don't. We *sometimes* have people here.

ALEX. How long is this one going to be?

PETER. A few days. A week, maybe.

ALEX. A week?

PETER. A week, yes.

ALEX. Why do you have to *do* that?? I hate it when people are here.

PETER. Why?

ALEX. It's too complicated. The house is full of obstacles.

PETER. Obstacles?

ALEX. Like at Christmas. Everywhere. Obstacles.

PETER. By *obstacles* do you mean visitors?

ALEX. Yes.

PETER. Relatives? Friends?

ALEX. Yes.

PETER. *Obstacles??*

ALEX. Yes. And now there's a new one.

PETER. A visitor.

ALEX. Unscheduled.

ALEX *turns and starts heading for the stairs – clearly pissed off –*

PETER. Alex –

ALEX. An unscheduled obstacle.

ALEX *starts heading up the stairs.*

PETER. It's just a nice woman, a *funny* woman. You'll like her, she'll make you laugh. *Alex!*

He disappears up the stairs.

As he disappears, the doorbell rings. PETER *checks out the front window to see who it is. Sags. Oh, not him!*

He opens the door – to reveal THE NEIGHBOUR. *A man in his sixties. Gray, lugubrious, relentlessly amiable and dull.*

THE NEIGHBOUR. Don't worry, I won't be a minute.

PETER. Okay.

THE NEIGHBOUR. Do you have a minute?

PETER (*dying for an excuse*). Um. Well. God! I mean, it's all go, isn't it –

THE NEIGHBOUR. Just a minute. That's all.

PETER. Well – okay, yes, yes, come in. Please.

Desperately trying to conceal his reluctance, PETER *ushers him in.*

THE NEIGHBOUR. I won't be long.

PETER. Oh, no, it's fine –

THE NEIGHBOUR. I won't even sit down. I know how busy you are.

PETER. Well that's entirely up to you, I don't mind. You can sit.

THE NEIGHBOUR. No, no. You're a busy man. Every time I talk to you, busy, busy. I can stand.

PETER. Up to you.

THE NEIGHBOUR. Middle of something, are you?

PETER. Well – just with Alex. We were discussing a few things, quite important. You know. That age.

THE NEIGHBOUR. Is he the one with the guitar?

PETER. Yes.

THE NEIGHBOUR. The electric guitar.

PETER. Yes, electric.

THE NEIGHBOUR. He's very keen, isn't he?

PETER. Yes.

THE NEIGHBOUR. I'm always hearing him. Playing away. All hours.

PETER. So what's the problem?

THE NEIGHBOUR. I was just wondering. After what we talked about yesterday. Have you had a chance to think about it?

PETER. Think about what?

THE NEIGHBOUR. What we talked about yesterday?

PETER. Um… well – which part?

THE NEIGHBOUR. Ha! I *thought* you weren't listening.

PETER. Oh, no, no, I was.

THE NEIGHBOUR. I said to Joan, he wasn't listening. You had that face – not listening. I know that face.

PETER. No, no, not at all, no.

THE NEIGHBOUR. Busy man, I completely understand –

PETER. I *was* listening.

THE NEIGHBOUR. Oh, good, good.

Painful pause.

So what did you think?

PETER.…Um. What about? Specifically.

THE NEIGHBOUR. The garden.

PETER. Right, yes. The garden. The garden.

THE NEIGHBOUR. Is it okay with you?

PETER. Um… I mean… you know… broadly…

THE NEIGHBOUR. Would you like me to explain again?

PETER. *Yes.* Yes, okay, why not? Just to… really nail it down.

THE NEIGHBOUR *goes to the back window.*

THE NEIGHBOUR. That wall there – between our gardens – which is my wall – is starting to collapse.

Behind him, PETER *reacts to a buzz from his phone. As* THE NEIGHBOUR *drones on,* PETER *gets out his phone, checks his texts…*

Now the wall is mine. But the quantity of soil pressing against it, and causing the collapse, is yours. So I wondered if we could split the repair costs.

He turns to look at PETER, *who is frowning at the text he just received. He looks up at* THE NEIGHBOUR.

PETER. Sorry. My wife just texted me. She wants me to google someone. Not really sure why she can't do it herself, but there you go.

THE NEIGHBOUR. So what do you think?

PETER (*realises he hasn't listened*)....um.

THE NEIGHBOUR. Were you listening? I can see you're on your phone.

PETER. No, no –

THE NEIGHBOUR. Always on your phone, aren't you? I see you sometimes, head down over your phone. In the sunshine.

PETER. No, no, it's not that – I was just trying to remember what you said yesterday, and I ended up... not... completely focusing...

THE NEIGHBOUR. Will I explain again?

PETER. Let's run it through one more time, yes.

THE NEIGHBOUR *turns to the window.* PETER *immediately looks back at the puzzling text on his phone*

THE NEIGHBOUR. If you look in the garden. The line between your garden and my garden.

Now as THE NEIGHBOUR *keeps talking, we hear a car drawing up outside.* PETER *goes to the front window who it is.*

The wall is our wall, but the damage to the wall is coming from your side of the garden. So could we split the repair costs?

He turns to PETER, *who is in the act of turning from the front window.*

What do you think?

Painful pause. PETER – *Shit! Didn't listen again!*

PETER....that's Debbie home.

THE NEIGHBOUR. Yes.

And THE NEIGHBOUR *just stands there, resolutely smiling and waiting for an answer.*

Bit early actually. Let's hope nothing's wrong.

THE NEIGHBOUR. Yes.

THE NEIGHBOUR *nods, smiles, waits.*

The car door bangs outside.

PETER. She sounds okay so far.

THE NEIGHBOUR. She always parks in your driveway, doesn't she, Debbie?

PETER. Well, of course –

THE NEIGHBOUR. You usually park in front of our house.

PETER. Well, it's not on purpose –

THE NEIGHBOUR. Oh, no, no –

PETER. I just park where there's a space –

THE NEIGHBOUR. That's what I tell Joan, when we're discussing it. He probably hasn't had time to clear his garage, he's a busy man.

PETER. Clearing it this weekend.

THE NEIGHBOUR. Oh, no rush, in your own time. So what do you think?

PETER. About what?

THE NEIGHBOUR. The garden. The situation. The garden situation.

PETER. Well. I think… I think I should really discuss this with Debbie.

THE NEIGHBOUR. Of course, yes.

PETER. It's not something I can really decide on my own.

THE NEIGHBOUR. Got to involve the little woman.

PETER. Well – my *wife*.

THE NEIGHBOUR. Your wife, yes. The little woman. I'll get out of your way and let you have a chat with her.

And just as THE NEIGHBOUR *starts towards the door,* DEBBIE *comes through it, clearly in a state of some agitation.*

DEBBIE. Did you do it? Did you google her?

PETER. Sorry, what?

DEBBIE. I texted you, I told Alex to tell you to google her – shitting hell, can't that boy remember *anything*??

(*Notices* THE NEIGHBOUR.) Oh, sorry –

THE NEIGHBOUR. I'm just leaving, Debbie, don't worry. Not getting in the way.

DEBBIE. Pardon my language.

THE NEIGHBOUR. No, no. I was just talking to your husband about a problem.

DEBBIE. Oh, dear, are you. What's up?

THE NEIGHBOUR. I'll let your husband explain.

PETER. Yes. I'll explain. Absolutely.

DEBBIE (*turns to* PETER). What is it? What's wrong?

PETER *on the spot again. And* THE NEIGHBOUR *has stopped leaving.*

PETER. Um. Well…

THE NEIGHBOUR. I hope you won't think I'm being cheeky.

DEBBIE. Cheeky about what?

THE NEIGHBOUR. Better if your husband explains the problem.

PETER.... You know, maybe Debbie and I should discuss this in private.

THE NEIGHBOUR. Yes. Sorry. Busy people.

DEBBIE. In private?

THE NEIGHBOUR. I'll get out of everybody's way.

PETER. It's a little bit...

He flounders for anything he can possibly say. He's just trying to fill in time for THE NEIGHBOUR *to get to the door.*

DEBBIE. Bit what?

PETER.... delicate.

THE NEIGHBOUR *turns in the doorway.*

THE NEIGHBOUR. Tell you what. I'll go and take a photograph of it.

He goes out.

DEBBIE. Photograph of what?

PETER. I have absolutely no idea. I can't retain anything he says – he's so boring he's actually memory-proof. The moment he breaks eye contact, I forget he exists.

ALEX (*from off*). Mum!

DEBBIE (*calling up stairs*). Hello, darling. I'm just talking to Dad.

PETER. Who am I supposed to google?

DEBBIE. Elsa.

PETER. Why?

DEBBIE. Because I just did.

ALEX (*from off*). Mum!

DEBBIE (*calling upstairs*). Alex, it's okay, I know you didn't give Dad the message, but I'm giving it to him now, okay?

A silence.

Okay?

ALEX (*from off*). Mum!

DEBBIE *sags.*

DEBBIE. Why can he only hear in one direction?

PETER. Headphones – he forgets he's wearing them. Why am I googling Elsa?

He's opened a laptop.

DEBBIE. No, actually, don't.

PETER. Don't what?

DEBBIE. Don't google her.

PETER. You just told me to.

DEBBIE. I changed my mind – you need to brace yourself first.

PETER. Why?

DEBBIE. Your blood pressure.

PETER. I'm permanently braced. That's the *reason* for the blood pressure.

ALEX (*from off*). Mum!

DEBBIE (*calling upstairs*). Alex, I'm talking to Dad now, it's all fine.

Silence.

It's all fine, did you hear me?

Silence.

Alex? Did you hear me?

ALEX (*from off*). Mum!

DEBBIE *sags*.

PETER. Brace myself for what?

DEBBIE. Okay. You know all these emails she's been sending. The questions.

PETER. Yeah.

DEBBIE. Are foxes the same as wolves? How much faster is time near Greenwich?

PETER. Is your house haunted? Please send a photograph of your kitchen! She's nuts, we knew that…

DEBBIE. Well today, on her Facebook, she put up our address.

PETER. She *what*??

DEBBIE. She just wanted all her friends to know exactly where she was staying.

PETER. Okay…

DEBBIE. In case, apparently, 'anything happened to her'.

PETER (*laughing*). Seriously.

DEBBIE. It's not funny.

PETER. It's a little bit funny.

DEBBIE. It's *not funny*.

She's serious. A moment between them.

ALEX (*from off*). Mum!

PETER. You know, I think he's winding down.

DEBBIE. Okay. So I thought, that's a bit weird. And then I thought, I know nothing about this woman we just invited into our home. Where we live our happy lives. With our kids.

PETER. So now you're being dramatic.

DEBBIE. I'm nowhere near dramatic yet. I'm moving towards dramatic. You'll know when I get there.

ALEX (*from off*). Mum!

DEBBIE. So – Elsa Jean Krakowski! I thought, how many of those can there be? I googled her. As it turns out, there's exactly one. Our one.

PETER. Right? And?

DEBBIE. What is the worst thing you could suddenly find out about someone who's coming to stay in your house for a week?

As PETER *ponders, there are feet on the stairs.*

ROSIE, *a teenage girl, is standing there, looking indignantly at them.*

ROSIE. Can't you hear that?

PETER. Hear what, darling?

ROSIE. He's just lying there. Going off, like a car alarm.

ALEX (*from off*). Mum!

ROSIE. See? Are you going to do something?

DEBBIE. In a minute, sweetie.

ROSIE. It's driving me mental.

PETER. Well, why don't you pop into his room, and just tell him that his mum and me –

ROSIE. Dad, don't be disgusting, I'm not going *inside* his room. I have to wash my hair if he leaves his door open.

DEBBIE. Darling, we're just in the middle of something important –

ROSIE. Oh, of course. Of course you are, I'm so sorry I accidentally exist.

PETER. Rosie –

ROSIE. Awesome parenting. Really awesome. I'm *so* grateful.

ALEX (*from off*). Mum!

ROSIE. Please, Mum, you've got to do something about that. Switch him off.

DEBBIE. Oh, are you giving me orders now, Rosie?

PETER. Now, you two, just leave it. He's slowing down anyway. He's been awake for about three hours now, he must be due another week's sleep.

ROSIE. You know what? You're selfish. That's the trouble with all of you, you're completely selfish. From now on, everyone in this family really needs to focus on how much their selfishness is affecting *me*.

She storms up the stairs.

PETER *and* DEBBIE, *alone again.*

PETER. Right. So tell me –

DEBBIE *puts her finger to her lips. Shh!*

DEBBIE. Rosie? Rosie, are you listening?

Silence.

Rosie, it's bad manners to listen.

Silence.

Rosie?

ROSIE *pokes her head round the top of the stairs.*

ROSIE. Are you talking about me?

DEBBIE. No. We're talking about something else. Now would you mind going to your room?

ROSIE. You're always keeping secrets from me.

DEBBIE. No, we're not. There are just some things in the world that happen to be none of your business.

ROSIE. Well isn't that *my* decision?

DEBBIE. No, if you think about it for a more than second, it really is not!

ROSIE *'humphs' and storms up the stairs.*

PETER. Do both our children hate us?

DEBBIE. Yes, but not as much as they hate each other, so they'll never win.

DEBBIE *considers a moment, then takes* PETER *by the arm and leads him into the kitchen, closing the connecting door to the living room. Clearly this is something they often have to do, to get out of earshot.*

PETER. Okay, so what's the worst thing you can find out about someone who's coming to stay?

DEBBIE. Guess.

PETER. No. Just tell me.

DEBBIE. No, I really want you to guess.

PETER. Debbie, if it's important, just –

DEBBIE. Guess.

PETER. I don't know. How would I know?

(*A flail.*) She's a… murderer.

DEBBIE. Yes.

PETER. I'm sorry?

DEBBIE. Yes.

PETER. What do you mean, yes?

DEBBIE. I mean Elsa Jean Krakowski is a murderer.

ALEX (*from off*). Mum!

ROSIE (*from off; angrier, more indignant*). *Mum!*

PETER. A murderer?

DEBBIE. Yes. A murderer.

PETER. What do you mean, a murderer?

DEBBIE. I mean a murderer.

PETER....what, professionally?

DEBBIE. Elsa Jean Krakowski murdered her father, her first husband, attempted to murder her second husband and probably murdered up to five other people. She's a murderer. She murders people. And she's coming to stay in our house.

And they just stand and stare at each other.

As the lights fade:

ALEX *(from off)*. Mum!

Now ROSIE's *head pops round the top of the stairs from her 'listening station'.*

ROSIE. *Mum!*

ALEX *(from off)*. Mum!

ROSIE. *Mum!*

Onscreen Video Clip

One of those American true crime cable documentaries. All overwrought narration and grainy photographs.

A photo of ELSA, *looking particularly squat and villainous.*

PRESENTER. Elsa Jean Krakowski. Pillar of the community. Church-goer, wife, daughter, mother. But is she also a... killer at large?

The words 'KILLER AT LARGE' are stamped across her photograph. Now a photo of a little house – mean, squalid, run-down. Clearly the scene of the worst kind of crime.

In November 2018, Elsa Jean's husband, Martin, went to his local police station, and begged for protection. He claimed his wife, Elsa Jean, was poisoning him. But more than that – he told the police he wasn't her first victim.

A photograph of an elderly man.

Picture of a small-town police station.

That night, while in police protection, Martin died of a sudden gastric illness This programme has since discovered that five other people known to Elsa, including her father, her first husband, and her sister, died of remarkably similar gastric illnesses.

A series of photographs of the first husband and the elderly ladies.

Insufficient evidence has been found to bring a case against her – but there seems little doubt that this woman is a killer at large.

The lights come up on:

Peter and Debbie's House

Some time later. PETER *and* DEBBIE *in the kitchen. They have the laptop open in front of them on the kitchen table.*

Or they would have, if they weren't both pacing.

PETER. We could say my mum's taken a turn for the worse.

DEBBIE. Your mum's fine.

PETER. She's fine but she's old, it's believable.

DEBBIE. Shut up, she's got years in her.

PETER. She's ninety-two – it's a cliffhanger at best.

DEBBIE. Peter!

PETER. Look, I love my mum, I want her to live forever. I'm just saying it's a believable lie, given her age. Every time she has to chew it's a lottery.

DEBBIE. We are not lying. We will email Elsa and tell her the truth.

PETER. But how do you put it? There's no etiquette for this – there's no thing people always say in these circumstances. 'Please don't come to our house, we think you're probably a murderer.'

DEBBIE. She'll be on a plane any minute – we have to send an email, we have to cancel. It's fine – people get cancelled, she'll understand.

PETER. Yeah, well cancelling people is sort of her thing.

DEBBIE. We don't have to be offensive, or aggressive – we have to be polite but firm.

PETER. I mean, how do you just bring up something like this? How do you work the conversation round?

DEBBIE. Focus.

PETER. I don't see how the police ever manage to arrest anyone.

DEBBIE. Peter, take it seriously.

PETER. How do you even say it. 'With regret, in light of some of your recent murdering…'

DEBBIE. This person is a killer. She's practically a serial killer. No, she *is* a serial killer. And if we don't manage to write an email – just *an email*, Peter, just one of those things you write every day – she'll be in our house, sitting at our table, and *talking to our children*.

PETER. Okay, yes, sorry.

DEBBIE. We have to be firm, unapologetic, and, if necessary, blunt. What have we got so far?

PETER *sits at the computer.*

PETER. I don't think it's very good.

DEBBIE. Just read it out.

PETER. It may not be blunt enough.

DEBBIE. Read it.

PETER. 'Dear Elsa, sorry for your recent loss'…

DEBBIE. Oh, Jesus. What's *wrong* with us?

PETER. Embarrassment. We lack the necessary social skills to avoid death.

DEBBIE. Okay. Start again. New email.

PETER. I've got an idea.

DEBBIE.…what?

PETER. Let's do it tomorrow.

DEBBIE. Why is that better?

PETER. It's just common sense – you should never solve a problem too early, in case it goes away by itself.

DEBBIE. It's just delaying the inevitable.

PETER. People always say that. But what else can you do with the inevitable??

DEBBIE. We're doing this now.

PETER. Okay, another suggestion.

DEBBIE. Is it as good?

PETER. Just listen, okay.

DEBBIE. I'm listening.

PETER. There's a possibility we might be overreacting.

DEBBIE. No, I really don't think we are.

PETER. No. Listen, listen. What I'm saying is… basically… we ride it out.

DEBBIE. Sorry, what?

PETER. We ride it out.

DEBBIE.…What does that mean?

PETER. We… you know… just keep it light. Keep it chatty. Keep her away from… food preparation.

DEBBIE. You mean… sorry… . actually let her come here?

PETER. I'm just floating it.

DEBBIE. She's a murderer. She's a *serial killer*.

PETER. She'll be in the spare room.

DEBBIE. *What difference does that make?*

PETER. Right at the other end of the landing.

DEBBIE. Peter…!

PETER. I'm just saying, we've got to be rational –

DEBBIE. She's dangerous.

PETER. Dangerous, yes… but let's keep it in proportion. She tends to kill people over a protracted period of time – she's only got a week with us.

DEBBIE. What are you saying? She might not have *time* to kill us?

PETER. Not on her current performance.

DEBBIE. Just shut up.

PETER. Yeah, fair enough.

DEBBIE. Any other bright ideas?

PETER. Let's do it tomorrow.

DEBBIE. That was your first idea.

PETER. Plan A is always best.

DEBBIE. She's getting on a *plane* tomorrow.

PETER. Do we know that?

DEBBIE. It's on her Facebook, look.

She's working at the laptop now.

She's got her whole itinerary somewhere, I saw it. Hang on.

(*Frowning now.*) It was here. Maybe she deleted it – why would she delete it…

PETER. You see? Facebook's got it right! That's what the real world needs.

DEBBIE. What?

PETER. An 'unfriend' button.

A ringing sound. DEBBIE *freezes,* PETER *looks nonplussed.*

DEBBIE. Oh Christ.

PETER. What's that?

DEBBIE. It's her, it's Elsa.

PETER. How?

DEBBIE. She saw we were active on Facebook, it can do video calls –

PETER. Turn it off!!

DEBBIE. I… I think…

PETER. Just *turn it off*!

PETER *randomly hits the keyboard –*

– and with a chime the call is answered.

On the screen above the stage, ELSA*'s beaming face appears. It's in the 'vertical slot' format, suggesting she's using a mobile phone.*

ELSA (*on-screen*). Hello, lovely people.

Instantly PETER *and* DEBBIE *are all smiles.*

PETER. Hello!

DEBBIE. Hello, Elsa!

PETER. Wonderful to see you.

Behind PETER *and* DEBBIE *– and unseen by them –* ALEX *is plodding down the stairs.*

ELSA (*on-screen*). Oh, look at your little faces. I could eat you both up.

PETER. Oh, don't do that. Don't eat us.

ELSA (*on-screen*). Listen, I'm sorry, I'm so, so sorry.

DEBBIE. Why are you sorry, Elsa?

ELSA (*on-screen*). I changed my plans. I should have told you, my plans have been unavoidably changed by forces beyond my control.

   PETER *and* DEBBIE – *a slight brightening. Good news on the way? Are they off the hook?*

   Behind PETER *and* DEBBIE *we see* ALEX *start to approach them.*

PETER. Oh?

DEBBIE. What's happening?

PETER. Are you not coming over now?

   ALEX *has come to a halt behind. Frowns in preoccupation. Raises his finger, as he did before. That look of concentration, as he considers a possible internal combustion.*

ELSA (*on-screen*). There have been mistakes and mix-ups and errors for which I can only apologise. And I now need to ask you an important question.

PETER. Okay?

ELSA (*on-screen*). Are you ready for an important question?

DEBBIE. We are quite used to your questions now, Elsa.

   ALEX *has turned and headed for the stairs. He contemplates them. Considering the hydraulic problem. Changes his mind, turns, heads to the door.*

ELSA. Well this is a big one. Because I have a question about your front door.

PETER. Okay. I'm sure we can handle it.

DEBBIE. What about our front door?

ELSA (*on-screen*). Could you just please tell me… is this it?

She revolves her phone –

– and see a very ordinary suburban front door. Just as it is opened and ALEX steps into close-up.

PETER *and* DEBBIE *leap to their feet in horror. Oh my God!! She's right outside.*

ALEX *looks puzzled for a moment, then –*

ALEX. Mum!

And suddenly ELSA is bustling into the room, phone still in her hand.

ELSA. Oh my God, your house. It's just like I imagined. No! It's *even tinier*.

DEBBIE.…Elsa?

ELSA. Debbie! Peter! I am so excited.

PETER. How… We didn't –

ELSA. Two days early. I know. I'll explain! Who is this handsome young man?

DEBBIE. Alex. Our son.

ELSA. You look very like a young man I used to know. Except he was a little older. He's dead now, so you'll catch up. Could you bring my bags in, Alex?

ALEX. I've got a hydraulic issue.

ELSA. You'll be fine.

ALEX – a little startled at receiving orders – starts bringing her bags in.

PETER. Look. Elsa, it's great to see you – but –

He looks, flailing, to DEBBIE.

DEBBIE. We… weren't expecting you. Yet.

ELSA. I know. Don't I know that? I'm sorry. Is it a problem?

DEBBIE. No, no!

PETER. No problem at all.

DEBBIE. Of course not.

ELSA. Oh, thank God!

> PETER *and* DEBBIE *look at each other. Why did they just do that?*

> Barnaby. Remember Barnaby?

DEBBIE. On the cruise, yes.

ELSA. With the one-eyed mom?

DEBBIE. We remember.

ELSA. And the gigantic daughter?

DEBBIE. Yes.

ELSA (*to* ALEX). I'm not being personal, but the size of this girl – you could cover a sofa, and have enough left over for curtains.

> *A little laugh from* ALEX. *A sort of single bark – as phlegmatic as his speech.*

> You see, you think that's funny. I don't think Barnaby got it. Now Barnaby, he lives in London now. And I thought, I'll come over, couple of days early, and stay with Barnaby. I get off the plane, I give the address to the taxi driver and he brings me here. And I'm looking at your house. And I'm thinking, what's going on here?! I thought Barnaby was *rich*!! Then I think, maybe I gave the driver the wrong address. Maybe this is Peter and Debbie's little house. But I don't want to ring a stranger's doorbell in London with all your urban violence and *EastEnders*. So I looked you up on Facebook and there you were. Isn't technology wonderful?

DEBBIE. Yes.

PETER. Tremendous.

ELSA. Now I got to ask. You got to be honest. I'm early, so just tell me – is it a problem me being here?

PETER *and* DEBBIE *go straight into host mode – like they can't control their 'good manners' reflex.*

DEBBIE. Not at all.

PETER. No problem.

DEBBIE. Why would it be a problem?

ELSA. You English, you're so polite. Give it to me straight. Really, have you got any kind of issue with me showing up like this?

PETER *and* DEBBIE *can't stop the gushing reassurance.*

DEBBIE. No.

PETER. *No.*

DEBBIE. Not at all.

ELSA. Thank you. *Thank you!* You are my true friends. And let me tell you, I've been through a lot of friends.

At the still-open door, THE NEIGHBOUR *has reappeared, holding up his phone.*

THE NEIGHBOUR. Excuse me. I've got a photograph.

PETER. Of what?

ELSA. And who is this handsome gentleman?

THE NEIGHBOUR. Sorry. Am I in the way?

PETER. No, no – this our friend. Elsa Jean Krakowski.

ELSA. From Denver.

PETER. Yes, from Denver. We met her on holiday.

THE NEIGHBOUR. Oh, they're always going somewhere exotic, these two. Every time a plane flies over, I say to Joan, that will be Peter and Debbie off somewhere exotic, leaving the rest of us to it.

ELSA. Ohh, you're a tiny bit passive-aggressive, aren't you?

THE NEIGHBOUR. Well, manners cost nothing.

   (*To* PETER.) Aren't you going to introduce me?

PETER. Yes, sorry. Elsa, this is…

   Terrible pause. He doesn't know.

   …our neighbour.

THE NEIGHBOUR. Doesn't he have a name?

   A terrible pause. PETER *doesn't know!! He just freezes.*

PETER. Oh, yes. Yes, he does.

THE NEIGHBOUR (*laughing*). He probably doesn't know it.
   That would be funny.

   PETER *laughs too. Just a little forced.*

   Ten years neighbours and he doesn't know my name.

PETER. Ten years. Imagine that!

   He shoots a desperate look at DEBBIE, *who gives desperate
   little shrug. They are rescued by:*

ELSA (*looks round*). Oh my God, who's this?

   ROSIE *is descending the stairs.*

DEBBIE. Oh, this is our daughter. Rosie. Rosie, this is Elsa
   Jean Krakowski.

ELSA. Look at you two. You could be sisters. Rosie, you could
   be twins. I'm serious. Rosie, you could be your mother's
   twin.

ROSIE (*bit thrown by that*)….really?

ELSA. Two peas in a pod. I can't even tell who's older.

ROSIE. *Really?*

ELSA. You must tell me your moisturiser. No wait.

   (*To* DEBBIE.) You tell me.

ROSIE. Hang on. What are those?

She's pointing at ELSA*'s bags.*

ELSA. Those are my bags, dear.

ROSIE. Are you coming to stay? Why does nobody tell me anything? Why is everything always a secret from me??

THE NEIGHBOUR. Well, Rosie, your mum and dad are very busy people, and they don't always have the time to get everything done.

ROSIE (*stares at him*).…who are you??

DEBBIE *rescues her.*

DEBBIE. Anyway! Elsa, what about Barnaby? Isn't he expecting you?

PETER. We can get you a car, if you need to get over there.

DEBBIE. Peter could even drive you.

ELSA. No.

PETER. No?

ELSA. Barnaby isn't expecting me.

PETER. Why not?

ELSA. I just called him. Out in the street, when I thought I was at the wrong house – he's not expecting me at all.

She smiles. A 'what-can-you-do?' smile.

He's dead.

Peter and Debbie's House

Morning.

PETER *and* DEBBIE.

DEBBIE *sits at one end of the sofa.*

PETER *stands in front of the fireplace.*

The arrangement seems strangely formal. They both look serious, preoccupied.

As the curtain rises, ELSA *is coming through the door. She is wearing a hideous velour jogging suit. She has a towel round her shoulders.*

ELSA. Morning, lovely people, morning, morning.

DEBBIE. Elsa, could we have a word with you please?

ELSA. Ohh, that sounds serious.

PETER. I'm afraid it is. Very serious.

He gestures her into the vacant armchair.

A little disconcerted, she sits in the chair.

PETER *and* DEBBIE *exchange a glance. Here it comes.*

DEBBIE. We googled you.

A silence. They just let that land.

The silence, grows, extends.

PETER. I think you know what we found.

ELSA *is silent. A little afraid.*

DEBBIE *pushes the laptop towards her, opens it up.*

On the screen above, we see what ELSA *sees.*

A close-up of her, as taken at a police station. She looks suitably murderous.

The headline reads: 'How many did she kill?'

A long, cold silence.

When ELSA *speaks her voice is flat and sad.*

ELSA. Oh. Oh my God.

PETER. We don't know what the truth of all this is, but it doesn't look too good, does it?

ELSA *looks at him, expressionless.*

Do you want to comment on it?

ELSA. No.

PETER. I didn't think you would.

DEBBIE. We're making no presumptions. Let's be clear about that. But the plain fact is, this is something you should have told us about. You are a guest in our house. Our children live here. We were entitled to know about all of this.

ELSA *bows her head. No answer to that either.*

You can't stay here. I'm sure you understand that. Our number-one priority is that we do not endanger our children. Is there anything you want to say?

ELSA *doesn't meet her eye. Briefly shakes her head.*

Then I think you should go and pack. We've made a list of hotels. Choose one, we'll call you an Uber. And that's the last contact we want with you, I'm afraid.

ELSA *buries her face in her hands.*

PETER *and* DEBBIE *exchange a look. It's all tougher than you'd think.*

PETER. As Debbie says, we're making no judgements. We read what we read, and you know what it was.

DEBBIE. We have two impressionable teenagers in this house, we have all the normal pressures of a working couple…

PETER. Also my mother has taken a turn for worse –

DEBBIE (*cutting across him*). You can't stay here. You should have told us about this – it was your choice not to. I'm sorry, but you have to leave immediately.

A silence. Then a deep, heartfelt sigh from ELSA.

ELSA. I'm embarrassed to ask. But I'm on a very tight budget. Could you possibly help me with the hotel room?

PETER. We've discussed that. We realised it might be a problem.

DEBBIE. Yes. We can help you with that. But you have to leave immediately.

ELSA *nods, sombre.*

ELSA. I appreciate it. You're good people, both of you.

She rises to her feet, bearing a new world of pain on her shoulders.

I'm very sorry to have caused you distress. I will... I'll get my things together.

PETER *and* DEBBIE *fail to meet her eye.*

In the silence that follows, ELSA *turns, heads solemnly up the stairs.*

Then a slight lighting change brightens the stage, and PETER *and* DEBBIE *visibly relax, as if dropping out of 'character'.*

DEBBIE. I think that would work, wouldn't it.

PETER. We just have to be blunt, plain and honest.

DEBBIE. Don't do the thing about your mum though.

PETER. I think it helps with the final push.

DEBBIE. I don't like you saying it.

PETER. It's just a little white lie.

DEBBIE. What, pretending your mum is dying? It's offensive.

PETER. Ninety-two! There's only so offended she could be!

There is a noise from outside – a step on the path.

DEBBIE. Okay. Ready?

PETER. Ready!

They have now assumed their positions from the top of the scene.

ELSA *coming through the door, again in her velour jogging suit, towel draped round her shoulders..*

ELSA. Morning, lovely people, good morning. Lovely neighborhood! So many little English people! I said good morning to everyone I saw – they were *terrified*.

DEBBIE. Elsa, could we have a word with you please?

ELSA. Ohh, she sounds serious. Doesn't she sound serious, Peter?

PETER. I'm afraid it is serious. Very serious.

He gestures her into the vacant armchair.

She makes no moves.

Would you mind sitting with us for a moment.

A little disconcerted, ELSA *sits in the chair. A slightly nervous smile.*

PETER *and* DEBBIE *exchange a glance. Here it comes.*

DEBBIE. We googled you.

A silence. They just let that land.

The silence, grows, extends.

PETER *opens his mouth to speak, but –*

ELSA. Why?

PETER.…I'm sorry?

ELSA. Why did you google me? Why would anyone google a person like that? It's so rude!

PETER. No it isn't.

DEBBIE. We were *not* being rude.

PETER. Not at all.

ELSA. Were you trying to find dirt on me?

DEBBIE. I promise you, we weren't –

PETER. We wouldn't do that.

ELSA. If you didn't like me, you just had to say – you didn't have to go looking for *reasons*.

PETER. But we *do* like you.

DEBBIE. We were just… checking.

ELSA. Why?

A moment of fluster between PETER *and* DEBBIE *– for a moment they've lost control of this.*

PETER. Well you were coming to stay in our house! We wanted to know a bit more about you.

ELSA. I felt we had made a connection. I *trusted* you.

PETER (*indignant*). We trust you, we do!

DEBBIE. Of course we do!

PETER and DEBBIE *look at each other – What the fuck did they just say??*

ELSA. Well it doesn't look a whole lot like it from here.

PETER makes a huge effort. He's going to be stern.

PETER. All right. All right, maybe that was a little untrusting. I accept that. But Elsa, as it turns out, maybe we weren't so stupid. We googled you. And I think you know what we found.

DEBBIE pushes the laptop towards ELSA, *opens it up.*

On the screen above, we see what ELSA *sees.*

A close-up of her, as taken at a police station. She looks suitably murderous.

The headline reads: 'How many did she kill?'

A long, cold silence.

ELSA. Oh! Oh my God! *Where did they get that photograph?*

PETER. Never mind the photograph –

ELSA. Look at that face! My neck! I'm like a turtle person!

PETER. Elsa –

ELSA. My chins! I've always been a martyr to my chins.

PETER. It's not about the photograph.

ELSA. I won't lie to you, Peter – under the velour, I'm chins all the way down.

PETER. If we could maybe focus on the text, for a moment –

ELSA. My husband used to say my body was like the underside of a caterpillar.

PETER. Elsa –

ELSA. I checked on YouTube, he had a point.

DEBBIE. Elsa, please –

ELSA. Segmented.

PETER *and* DEBBIE *sag – How do you get through this??*

But that's getting older for you. Isn't that right, Debbie? One minute everything's pointing up, the next you're nothing but folds.

(*To* PETER.) As your wife and I have discovered, there's no way to halt the ageing process.

PETER. Well there's one way, and according to this website, you're pretty well acquainted with it.

ELSA. I'm not sure I follow what you mean, Peter.

PETER. Look, I'm fairly certain you've read this article.

ELSA. Sure, yeah.

PETER. You know what it says.

ELSA. Yeah.

PETER. It doesn't look too good, as I'm sure you realise.

ELSA *looks at him, expressionless.*

I mean, I'm making no judgements. But as your hosts, as parents of teenagers, at a highly impressionable age, this is really something we needed to know. Elsa, you should have told us.

ELSA *stares at him for a moment. A tear leaks from her eye. She reaches and takes his hand. In a quavery voice, she says:*

ELSA. Thank you.

PETER....for what?

ELSA. Making no judgements. That is so rare. That is *special*.

PETER*'s hand now being clung to.*

PETER. Yes. Yes, well...

A despairing look at DEBBIE. PETER *makes a slight attempt to detach. Fails.*

ELSA. *No judgements*. People judge me all the time. *All* the time. But not you, Peter! Not you!

ELSA *is now starting to sob. Big whoops.*

PETER. So. Um.

More whoops. And she isn't letting go.

Um.

Despairs again at DEBBIE. *A shrug from* DEBBIE, *and she eggs him on.*

Do you want to comment on this?

ELSA *whoops*.

Any of this?

ELSA *whoops*.

This situation. Any comments? Any… comment you want to make?

ELSA. Yes!

PETER. Okay.

ELSA. *You are a beautiful person!*

PETER. Right. Yes. Good then.

ELSA. You are, you know! You are a beautiful soul, Peter Lindel.

PETER.…thank you.

DEBBIE *now looking cross at him. For fuck's sake!*

PETER *pulls himself together – though his hand is still gripped by* ELSA.

But that's not, in fact, what I was asking. As I'm sure you realise, I was referring to the content of the website I just showed you. Do you have any reaction to that website?

ELSA. Yes! Yes, I do.

PETER. What?

ELSA. I'm against it.

PETER. Okay, but… you know, any *more* detail?

ELSA. I don't like it one bit.

PETER. Right. Good. Noted. But this website does kind of suggest… that you do seem to be… you know… implicated in six separate…

Can't say the word. DEBBIE *eggs him on.*

…incidents.

DEBBIE *despairs. Mouths 'Incidents??' at him.*

Involving... end-of-life... care.

DEBBIE (*mouthing*). *Care??*

PETER. But possibly a bit too... proactively.

DEBBIE (*mouthing*). *Jesus!*

   PETER *makes a Herculean effort to overcome his good manners.*

PETER. Elsa. There are a lot of people online who say you're a serial killer.

ELSA (*still sobbing*). I know. It's very upsetting.

PETER. I'm sure it is.

ELSA. Thank you for that. Oh my God, *thank you*!

PETER. But the fact remains, there have been a few... arguably more than a few... well, murders.

ELSA. There are two sides to every story.

PETER. Well, as it stands, there would have to be two sides to six stories.

ELSA. I know, isn't it awful? It's like I'm living under some kind of curse. No one understands. Not even my family.

PETER. In fairness, quite a few of them are dead.

ELSA. I *know*, it's like a nightmare.

PETER. Six nightmares. No, but seriously, how do you explain six people dying?

ELSA. Well I don't want to go pointing any fingers... but they were all vaccinated.

   PETER *looks to* DEBBIE. *How the hell does he do this?*

PETER. Elsa... I need to tell you about my mum.

DEBBIE. *Peter!*

He falls silent, chastened. DEBBIE *takes over.*

Elsa, please listen. Our primary concern is for our children. You know what's on that website. You know what we read. You understand, I'm sure, that before coming to stay with us, you should have told us about the stories online concerning you. Now, let me be clear – we are reacting as concerned parents *only*. We are making no presumptions about you or what happened to any of those six people –

ELSA. *No presumptions!* Bless you, Debbie!

She now grabs hold of DEBBIE's *hand. Both* PETER *and* DEBBIE *are now trapped by her.*

You two are the most wonderful souls in the world. I have waited a long, long time to hear the healing words of your understanding and forgiveness. God speaks through you both. I don't know what to say.

DEBBIE....No. No, apparently neither do we.

Through the front door, comes ALEX. *He's also dressed for jogging and has a towel round his shoulders.*

ALEX. I'm home.

ELSA (*a joyous cry*). So am I!

DEBBIE. Alex, sorry, we're just in the middle of something quite important –

(*Stops, staring.*) Where have you been?

ALEX. Jogging.

DEBBIE. Jogging??

ALEX. Yeah. Jogging.

PETER....outside?

ALEX. Of course, outside.

PETER. Really?

ALEX. Why wouldn't I be outside?

DEBBIE. We weren't sure you remembered where it was.

PETER. You told us once that *Grand Theft Auto 5* counted as exercise.

ALEX. Multiplayer.

ELSA (*puts her hand*). Guilty!

   PETER *and* DEBBIE *startle at this sudden admission.*

   Guess I got him out there. We were talking last night, weren't we, Alex?

PETER. Talking?

ELSA. He was on his computer. Playing games. That right, buddy?

ALEX. Yeah. There was tournament. Online. I've got some friends in Poland. I think they're Polish. Or Mexican.

ELSA. A violent game. Very violent.

   (*To* PETER *and* DEBBIE.) You two should have a look at the violent game he's playing up there.

ALEX. You liked it.

ELSA. Yeah, maybe.

ALEX. You were good at it.

ELSA. I like a bit of trouble, Alex. You know me.

   They laugh together, like old friends.

   PETER *and* DEBBIE *exchange a look. What??*

ALEX. Scared the hell out of those Mexican Polacks.

ELSA. Oh, trust me, this old girl can scare people.

DEBBIE. Sorry – he let you on his computer?

PETER. Actually *touch* it.

DEBBIE. And you *wanted* to?

ELSA. We had a fine old time. Didn't we, Alex? But then I said, you need some fresh air. I said, Alex, fresh air doesn't kill people!

(*To* PETER *and* DEBBIE.) Trust the expert, right?

(*To* ALEX.) Your mum and dad will tell you. I *love* fresh air!

ALEX *raises his finger, in the familiar way.*

ALEX. Speaking of which…

PETER. Alex, please, we're in the middle of a serious discussion –

ALEX. I'm not responsible for the timing. If you want me to leave, okay –

ELSA. Timing of what?

PETER. He's – Never mind.

ELSA. Timing of what, Alex?

ALEX. I've got a fart coming.

ELSA. Oh. Breaking wind. That's what we say in English.

ALEX. My mum and dad don't like when I… break wind downstairs, so I'll have to go.

PETER. We'll see you in a bit, Alex.

ALEX. Later.

ALEX *starts heading for the stairs.*

ELSA *watches him go.*

ELSA. Hey. Buddy?

ALEX *turns.*

Before you go, I just wanna say… bullshit.

ALEX. …sorry, what?

ELSA. You heard me. Bullshit. What you said. Bullshit. From your mouth to God's ears – bullshit.

ALEX. …what?

ELSA *is heaving herself up from the sofa now.*

ELSA. I understand your wind issues. Most days I'm living in a toxic mist. Birds fall dead from the sky, you know what I'm saying? But, Alex – bullshit.

ALEX....no. No, it's true. The moment I come down here, they find a reason to send me straight back up –

ELSA. Buddy – bullshit.

ALEX, finally silenced.

The moment you come down here, you find a way to make them send you back up. Because you want to go play on your computer with the Mexicans. But you tell yourself it's all Mom and Pop's fault, right?

ALEX....well... sometimes I really actually –

ELSA. Sometimes? Sure. But mostly? Bullshit.

For a moment, ALEX *looks like he's about to protest.*

Then he smiles sheepishly.

ALEX. Okay.

ELSA. You can't bullshit a bullshitter. Am I right?

ALEX. Okay, you're right.

ELSA. Now, maybe what you want to say is, sorry, I'd like to go play on my computer, but I will be down later to talk to you all. I kinda hope you're gonna say that, because I would like to talk to you later. How about you give that a go, big guy?

With a visible effort – but as pleasantly as he can – ALEX *addresses his parents.*

ALEX. Mum, Dad, I'm going to go and play on my computer. But I will be down later for a chat.

PETER *and* DEBBIE *stare – they've been staring for a while. Finally they remember to reply.*

PETER. Yes, fine.

DEBBIE. See you.

ALEX. Later.

ALEX starts heading for the stairs again.

ELSA. Buddy?

ALEX turns.

We talked all night. We fought Mexicans, we've been jogging. You just leaving me now?

(*Spreads her arms, as for a hug.*) Bring it in.

As PETER and DEBBIE watch in astonishment, ALEX goes to ELSA and gives her a big, big hug.

PETER *and* DEBBIE *look at each other. What. The. Fuck????*

That's enough, big guy. Don't want to squeeze too hard, you might go off.

With a laugh, ALEX starts to head up the stairs.

ALEX. Dad.

PETER. Yes?

ALEX. What I said about obstacles, yeah?

PETER. Yes.

ALEX. I didn't mean Elsa. Elsa can stay.

And he disappears up the stairs, leaving an entirely silenced PETER and DEBBIE.

ELSA walks back over and plonks herself down on the sofa, where she was before.

ELSA. Now then. What were we talking about?

A moment of uncertainty – then –

DEBBIE. The thing is… the problem here… I don't exactly know how to put this…

A desperate silence.

…Peter's mum is dying.

PETER.... Yes. Yes, she is. Dying. She's dying.

DEBBIE. It's been very difficult for all of us.

PETER. We just need to gather together as a family at this difficult time. I really hope you understand.

ELSA. You poor lovely people. Oh, why didn't you say something?

PETER. Well, you know, it's... difficult.

ELSA. You don't have to tell me. Oh, the people I've lost. I don't have time to tell you about the losses I've endured.

PETER. Well, we've seen the website.

DEBBIE. So – in view of that – I think you can see we need time, alone, as a family to process this.

ELSA. You don't have to say another word – this old girl is getting out of your way!

ROSIE (*from off*). *Oh my God!!*

They turn, to see ROSIE *putting her head round the top of the stairs from her listening post.*

Nana Jess? She's ill? I didn't know she was ill. *Why did nobody tell me she was ill??*

DEBBIE. She's not, she's not ill.

ROSIE. You just said she's dying. I heard you talking!

DEBBIE. No, no, she isn't dying – she's just... well, not *ill* as such... she's not dying or ill, she's just a little... Peter, you explain.

ROSIE. Dad?

PETER. Um...

ROSIE. I mean, why would you say Nana Jess is dying if she's not dying? Is she dying??

PETER. Well... she's not *dying* dying.

ROSIE.…what?

PETER. It's more… nuanced.

ROSIE. Oh, I get it. You're just making it up as an excuse to get rid of her.

She points rudely at ELSA, *who is listening with interest.*

DEBBIE. Rosie, don't you dare be so rude to our guest!

PETER. Of course we're not making it up.

ROSIE. It's true then? About Nana?

PETER. Well, it's more sort of… you know… *true.*

He pronounces 'true' as if it was an incredibly delicate equivocation.

ROSIE. I don't understand.

ELSA. Rosie Lindel, this is none of my damn business, and you can tell me to shut my big silly mouth if you want – but I know your father and mother, and I know what good, kind, decent people they are. There is no possibility, none at all, that they would tell a lie, about a beloved parent, as an excuse. And I think, if you look inside your heart, you'll see that you know that to be true.

ROSIE, *sulky, resentful.*

ROSIE. Sometimes, Dad will say anything if he thinks I'm too stupid to understand.

ELSA *rises from the sofa, crosses to* ROSIE, *takes her hands in hers.*

ELSA. Maybe what you need to do, my dear, is think about how your father might be feeling right now.

ROSIE *considers, chastened.*

PETER. Look… this really isn't completely necessary…

ELSA. Rosie, is there anything you want to say to your old dad? Because, I'll tell you something about parents you need to remember: you don't get to keep them forever.

PETER. Really, this isn't – I don't need –

ROSIE. Thank you, Elsa. Really, thank you.

ELSA. Don't you think there's an old guy standing over there you ought to be giving a hug right about now?

PETER. I'm basically fine.

ROSIE *goes to* PETER *and gives him a huge hug.*

PETER *is dying – he so doesn't deserve this – and so is* DEBBIE. *How to get control of this?*

Honestly, everything's okay, it's really fine. I'm fine, actually.

ELSA. Peter, I think you ought to tell Rosie about your mother. You've been brave enough. Let your daughter help you for once. You're about to lose one of the most important people in your life.

PETER. Oh, it's no bother.

ROSIE. It's all right, Dad, I can take it. I'd rather know.

ALEX. Know what?

They look round. ALEX *has come plodding down the stairs.*

PETER. Why don't we talk about this tomorrow, in case it… blows over.

ROSIE. In case what blows over. In case Nana blows over?

ALEX. Nana?

ROSIE. Something's wrong with Nana.

ALEX *considers this, solemnly. Pronounces judgement.*

ALEX. Fuck.

PETER. It's nothing. Well not *nothing* – sort of half nothing…

ALEX. Nana?

ROSIE. Yeah. Something's happened.

ALEX. …Fuck.

DEBBIE. Look, we don't have to talk about this now –

ALEX. Shitting fuck.

DEBBIE. Your father is just –

ALEX. Nana!

DEBBIE. Your father is having some very complicated feelings –

ALEX. Which Nana?

ROSIE. The one we call Nana.

ALEX. I thought we called them both that.

ROSIE. Dad's mum.

DEBBIE. We'll talk it all through with you both tomorrow –

ELSA. You know what the problem is here? Me! This is a family matter. Elsa Jean Krakowski is gonna get out of your damn way.

PETER. Okay!

ROSIE. No!

(Puts a hand on ELSA's.) You're helping. You really are.

ALEX. Yeah. Elsa can stay.

PETER *and* DEBBIE *exchange a despairing glance.*

ALEX *has now descended the stairs, joining them.*

In what is clearly a momentous move, ROSIE *takes* ALEX's *hand.*

ROSIE. Dad… what's going on?

PETER. Well. It's complicated.

ROSIE. We're listening.

PETER *takes a moment. How the hell does he negotiate the rapids of this explanation?*

PETER. Okay. I went to see Nana this morning, and although she was up bright and early, and perfectly healthy and happy so there's absolutely nothing for either of you two to worry about... I also somehow got a general sense, a slight, nagging feeling that she might suddenly... just... die.

(*Off their horrified stares.*) Just a feeling. Just a sort of... intuition.

A slightly dazed silence.

ALEX. Fuck.

ROSIE. You had an intuition that your mother was about to die?

PETER. Who can say where these feelings come from?

ROSIE....So you came straight home?

PETER *grapples with the logic of that one for a moment.*

PETER. I thought she'd rather be alone.

ROSIE. *Why didn't you stay with her?*

PETER. Well – she was just lying there.

ALEX. You said she was up.

PETER. Sorry, what?

ALEX. Up bright and early, you said.

PETER....Well, yes, she was up. She wasn't lying in *bed*, she was just sort of lying... about.

ROSIE....Where?

PETER. Oh, you know. The living room, I think.

ROSIE. You *think*??

PETER. It was fine. She seemed really comfortable.

ROSIE. But unconscious?

PETER. I'd say more sleeping.

ROSIE. On the *floor*?

PETER. It was strangely peaceful.

ROSIE. *Are you even sure she was alive??*

PETER. Oh, no, she was. I could hear her... moaning.
Contentedly. Well, it was more of a sort of gentle humming
really. A happy humming. But, you know... slowly tailing
off. Fairly slowly. So nothing to immediately worry about
but possibly with a slight hint of finality.

An entirely incredulous silence. ROSIE *just stares at him.*

PETER *is psychologically exhausted. He practically flops.*

ROSIE. And you came home and told all this to Mum?

PETER. Yes. Didn't I, darling? I explained it all to Mummy.

DEBBIE, *staring at him, not wanting to be part of this.*

DEBBIE....yes.

ROSIE. And what did you say?

DEBBIE. Well. One hardly knew where to start.

ELSA *rises majestically from the sofa.*

ELSA. Peter, you're upset, you're not thinking clearly. Go to
your mother. Go to her, Peter.

PETER (*looking at watch*). Oh, um... now?

ELSA. Debbie, you'd better drive. He's not in a fit state. Please
go and spend time with your mother, Peter.

PETER. Wouldn't it be better to leave her alone for a bit and see
if she recovers?

ROSIE. *Dad!*

PETER. It's a long way...

DEBBIE. We can't leave the kids –

ROSIE. We're not kids.

ELSA. Don't you worry about a thing. Elsa Jean Krakowski is
here to help. I'll look after these kids like they were my very
own.

PETER *and* DEBBIE *are now frozen in horror.*

What are you waiting for? Go! *Go!*

ROSIE. Mum! Dad! You've got to go.

PETER *and* DEBBIE *find themselves hesitating to their feet.*

ELSA *is now standing between* ROSIE *and* ALEX. *She puts her arms round them.*

ELSA. We're gonna get through this, people. Nothing brings a family together like tragedy – and nobody knows that like me. Tell you what: I'm gonna cook us all dinner!

End of Act One.

ACT TWO

Peter and Debbie's House

THE NEIGHBOUR *is sitting on the sofa. He is very still and patient. Almost blank. Like he powers down when alone.*

A long silence. Sits and sits. A pause of theatrically scary proportions.

Then:

We hear a car pass outside.

THE NEIGHBOUR *turns his head to the window – keeps slowly turning his head as the car passes the house. The only action we've seen so far.*

The car is gone. THE NEIGHBOUR *faces front again. The stillness resumes. The silence. The sitting.*

From upstairs. A creak of a floorboard.

THE NEIGHBOUR *looks up. A toilet flushes. Creaks as someone upstairs walks across a floor.* THE NEIGHBOUR's *head turns, following. A door closes. Stillness.*

Distantly, a clock is chiming.

THE NEIGHBOUR *looks at his watch, gives the slightest nod of satisfaction. Faces front again.*

Now we hear a car draw up outside, stop, switch off. Footsteps as someone climbs out. A car door bangs.

We hear a voice from outside – PETER's.

PETER (*from off*). No, I did. I don't know why, I just did.

PETER *coming through the door, talking on his mobile. He has two plastic bags – one clearly from a wine shop, the other from a bookshop. He seems breezy, cheerful – a happier* PETER *than we're used to.*

Maybe I was relaxed. Yeah, I think I'm actually relaxed.
I drove for hours. Just for the hell of it. I went and saw
Alistair – without texting first. Without *texting*. I mean when
was the last time I even spoke to anyone without texting
them in advance? It was crazy! It was like the sixties! I went
to the *park*! Dropped in on Sheila, who's fine by the way,
sends her love. Dropped in on you, but you were out. Drove
some more, bought wine, went to a bookshop – two hours
there, *two hours* – came home.

(…)

I dunno. I told you, I think I'm *relaxed*.

(…)

It was just an impulse. I just went out to the garage, and there
was the car and I thought, what the hell. Day off – why not
just go somewhere? I mean, what was I even doing in the
garage, I don't know! No, hang on, it was boring-bastard next
door. He came round asking about some photo he'd sent to me
and I realised I'd left my phone in the car. And of course he
insisted on waiting around while I went and… found…

Starting to dawn on him now.

…it.

Oh shit.

He slowly turns –

– and sees THE NEIGHBOUR, *sitting there. Ever so
patiently.*

THE NEIGHBOUR. Did you manage to have a look at the
photograph?

PETER (*into phone*). Sorry, got to go. Love you, Mum.

(*Hangs up.*) I am so, so, so sorry –

THE NEIGHBOUR. I understand.

PETER. I have no idea how I managed to do that. That was
incredibly rude and thoughtless.

THE NEIGHBOUR. You're a busy man.

As he says this, PETER *is putting his bags on the table. One of them clinks – the unmistakeable sound of wine bottles.*

You certainly like your wine, don't you?

PETER. Well, yes, I suppose we do –

THE NEIGHBOUR. Don't be modest, I know I'm living next to a couple of proper wine connoisseurs – I can always hear you putting out the recycling.

PETER. Okay.

THE NEIGHBOUR. It goes on and on, doesn't it. We have to pause the television.

PETER. We like a glass of wine, I suppose –

THE NEIGHBOUR. Oh, I know you've got it firmly under control, don't get me wrong. Joan and I have discussed it at length.

PETER. Have you? Good-oh.

THE NEIGHBOUR. I would have aired the subject before now if we were worried about the levels.

PETER. Well I wasn't actually aware that our recycling was a subject of neighbourhood discussion –

THE NEIGHBOUR. Don't you worry about that… What's on WhatsApp *stays* on WhatsApp.

PETER.…anyway. Sorry. You really didn't have to wait all this time for me.

THE NEIGHBOUR. And I knew you'd be back, once you'd got all your wine. And Elsa made me lots of cups of tea.

PETER. Well, good.

THE NEIGHBOUR. Tea is for me what wine is for you. But without the behavioural aspects.

If you can nod through gritted teeth, PETER *is doing that.*

PETER. Where *is* Elsa?

THE NEIGHBOUR. Oh, she'll be about somewhere I expect. She's a busy one, Elsa, isn't she? Joan and I are always saying – Peter and Debbie keep that old lady run off her feet with all their comings and goings.

PETER. Well, I don't think we actually – I mean, we're not *employing* her –

THE NEIGHBOUR. Anyway, I'd better not keep you from your evening.

He says this while gesturing vaguely at the bag of wine bottles.

PETER. See you soon.

THE NEIGHBOUR. But did you have time to look at the photo?

PETER. What photo?

THE NEIGHBOUR. About the garden situation? The one I sent to your phone? You went out to your car for your phone, remember –

PETER. Right, yes, yes, of course I remember, yes!

(*Scrolling through phone.*) Can't seem to find the email…

THE NEIGHBOUR. I did send it.

PETER. Could you send it again?

THE NEIGHBOUR. Twice.

PETER. …maybe I should check in the junk mail, I'm always losing stuff, I don't know why – maybe I've been hacked –

THE NEIGHBOUR. I'll send it again, shall I?

PETER. Would you mind?

THE NEIGHBOUR (*working at his mobile*). Not at all. I'll send it right now. It'll be on your phone before I'm even out this door. Not unlike yourself, Peter.

He chuckles at his own joke. PETER *does the worst forced laugh ever.*

(*As he leaves.*) Oh, we have a laugh, don't we?

And he's gone. PETER *stands there a moment. God, he hates that man –*

– his phone beeps. He reaches to pull it out his pocket –

– and the doorbell rings. He steps to the door, opens it. And there's his smiling NEIGHBOUR.

I've just sent it. Maybe you should have a look now, before you get too busy.

PETER. Yes, yes, I will, don't worry.

THE NEIGHBOUR. I don't like being a burden like this.

PETER. No, no, you're not a burden, I'll get right to it.

THE NEIGHBOUR. Tell you what. I'll come back in five minutes, and we'll have a little chat.

PETER. Yes, great.

THE NEIGHBOUR. Do you think you'll have time to glance briefly at a photograph in the next five minutes.

PETER. I'll try and squeeze it in.

THE NEIGHBOUR. That would be very considerate. Thank you, Peter.

He closes the door on THE NEIGHBOUR. *As he heads toward his plastic bags, waiting on the table, he's already pocketing his phone.*

But no! He remembers – pulls his phone out –

– just as ALEX *comes down the stairs. He is wearing cycling clothes and a cycling helmet.*

PETER *stares at him, the phone forgotten.*

ALEX *reaches the foot of the stairs, smiles pleasantly back at him.*

PETER. Where are you going?

ALEX. Cycling.

PETER. *Cycling?*

ALEX. Bit of exercise.

PETER. You've got all the gear then.

ALEX. Online. What do you think?

PETER. Very nice.

ALEX. Spent ages choosing. The gloves have special heated ridges. Look. And see that panel in the forefinger? You can use your phone. And the shoes, they attach to the pedals, so you're not just pushing down, you're pulling up too.

PETER. Did you get a bike?

A slightly embarrassed silence.

You realise you actually have to *have* a bike, don't you? They don't just happen. It's not an upgrade you get if you go outside in a helmet.

ALEX *stares at him in puzzlement for a moment –*

– then bursts out laughing.

ALEX. You really think I'm an idiot, don't you? There's a bike in the garage.

PETER. My old one.

ALEX. Yeah.

PETER. It's ancient.

ALEX. Elsa helped me do it up.

PETER. You and Elsa did up my old bike.

ALEX. Is that okay?

PETER. Of course it's okay, it's great.

ALEX. Thanks, Dad.

And to PETER*'s astonishment* ALEX *comes over to him, gives him a hug. Then detaches, heads to the door.*

Love you.

He goes out.

PETER *stares at the door, after it's closed.* Wow! Big change there.

Oh! The phone in his hand. He raises it, but –

Laughter from outside – ROSIE.

Now ROSIE *comes bouncing through the door. Bags full of shopping, including some cut flowers.*

ROSIE. Hey, Dad!

PETER. What's funny?

ROSIE. Oh, just Alex being Alex. He's a funny guy, isn't he?

PETER. Yes, I suppose he is. Good to see you two getting on.

ROSIE. What are you talking about? We *always* get on.

She's gone through to the kitchen. Starts arranging the flowers in a vase. PETER *follows her through.*

PETER. So what have you been up to?

ROSIE. Oh, I just went to the mall.

PETER. The mall?

ROSIE. Yeah. With my friends.

PETER. You mean the shops.

ROSIE. The mall, yeah.

She is busily arranging the flowers now.

PETER. Flowers?

ROSIE. For the living room. Just to brighten things up, yeah? Mum loves flowers. Do you love flowers?

PETER. How does anyone actually love flowers? They are literally vegetables for looking at.

ROSIE *roars with laughter at this – and hugs him. He is mildly astonished at the display of affection.*

ROSIE. Love you, Dad.

She breaks from him, picks up the vase of flowers, takes it through to the living room.

Elsa says you should always have something living in the house.

PETER. Well, those are cut flowers. Which is consistent at least.

ROSIE. How long is she staying?

PETER. It was supposed to be a week, but I don't see any sign of her packing.

ROSIE. I don't mind.

PETER. Does she ever... talk to you? About her past?

ROSIE. She's had so much tragedy in her life. But she keeps smiling through. She knows how to be happy. You should follow her example.

PETER. Well, that would be... controversial.

ROSIE. See you in a bit.

ROSIE *grabs her shopping, heads up the stairs.*

PETER *is bemused for a moment. Shakes his head. He notices the plastic bag of wine bottles.*

He picks up the bag, heads through to the kitchen. He is about to put the bottles in the wine rack, when he finally remembers!

He pulls out his phone to look at the photograph –

– and at that exact moment –

The back door (leading to the back garden) opens. Stepping through it is a portly uniformed policemen. This is PC JUNKIN. He is affable, slow, pleasant. Everything he does is an amble.

PETER *stares. What??*

PC JUNKIN *barely registers* PETER's *presence – just a brief nod.* PC JUNKIN *goes to the fridge, opens it. He takes out a half-full bottle of milk. Sniffs it. Frowns slightly. Sniffs it again. Ew! Bit off. He puts it back, takes out another, fresh milk bottle. Opens it, sniffs. Clearly better! He's about to close the fridge, when he notices something else.*

He reaches into the fridge, takes a banana, pockets it. Again, he's about to close the fridge, and notices something.

He reaches in and takes a slice of a cake that's sitting there on a plate. Sniffs it, considers. Nah. Puts it back.

Finally, he closes the fridge. He nods briefly to PETER *again, ambles calmly out the back door, and closes it behind him.*

A silence as PETER *just stares. What the fuck was that??*

Then the back door opens again, and ELSA *sticks her head through.*

ELSA. I'll explain in a moment.

She withdraws, closing the door.

PETER *stares for a moment. What? What??*

He steps towards the door, when –

– the front door flies open. Now storming into the room is DEBBIE. (*As she comes storming in, she doesn't completely close the door when she slams it.*)

DEBBIE. I've had enough! Peter, seriously, enough! She's a murderer. *She's a murderer!* And we're too polite to bring it up. We're dying of manners. We're under siege from personal embarrassment. This is not sane. This is not rational. That woman is a monster! She's a cold-hearted killer who killed members of her own family. Her father! Her sister. At least three old ladies! One-and-a-half husbands. And we've let her stay in our house for *six days*. That's a day per victim! She's a serial poisoner and we let her *cook for our family*! We sit there, saying 'no you have the first bite!' That is *not* an adequate safety precaution. That falls short of due diligence! That is an affront to health and safety! And why? Why?? Because we can't find a way to say 'No, please don't cook for us, Elsa, you have a substantive history of poisoning people to death!' Because it might hurt her feelings. How did this happen? How did we get here? We've got a serial killer as a houseguest – a certifiable psychopathic monster – and every day, somehow, it matters a tiny bit less. Piece by piece, it's more and more okay. It's our new normal. Like you just have to hang around with a mass murderer long enough, and you start thinking 'Hey, we've all got our irritating mannerisms.' Less than a week, and we're starting to be okay with the deliberate, planned murder of the innocent. Just *six days* and we're accepting her. Give it a year, we'll be voting for her! And you know what the worst part is?? She's nice! People love her! Our kids love her. She's made this home a better place. Rosie is communicating with us in something other than a permanent state of offence. Alex is actually leaving the house and exercising. You are phoning and visiting your mother, instead of just using her as an all-purpose excuse – and all that's down to Elsa. She's the killer who came to stay – and every day she's improving our lives. She's Murder Poppins! Everyone in the street adores her. She's the most popular human being I've ever met. But she *kills* people! She kills people and she's *popular*! *That's not fair*. It's not fair, Peter. I've gone through my entire life not killing people. I thought that was what you were supposed to do. That's what they told us! I've got friends, I've got family – and I have spent many, many years very specifically *not killing* any of them. You think I didn't want to? I'm human! I've got feelings. Anthea! You've met Anthea! I have spent day after day *not killing* Anthea. Do you think that was easy?? A person *burns calories* not killing Anthea. And where's the gratitude? What do I get for that? I get called uptight. That's what people call me. Uptight. Elsa's popular, and I'm uptight. Of course I'm uptight – *I'm not allowed to kill anyone*. Nothing in my life makes sense. Since that woman stepped through our door, nothing has

made sense. And you just stand there, gawping at me. Say
something. Please, just make some of this make sense. For
Christ's sake – for once in your life – *say something*!

PETER....there's a policeman in the garden stealing our milk.

The doorbell rings and THE NEIGHBOUR *pops his head
round the partly opened door.*

THE NEIGHBOUR. Peter, did you find time to glance at that
photograph?

PETER. Oh! Christ! Sorry!

THE NEIGHBOUR. You're a busy man.

PETER. It's just, you know, one of those days –

THE NEIGHBOUR. Shall I give you another five minutes?

PETER. That would be great –

THE NEIGHBOUR. It'll only take a second. You just have to
glance at it.

PETER. I will. I'll glance.

THE NEIGHBOUR. Just before your evening gets started.
Hello, Debbie.

DEBBIE. Hello.

THE NEIGHBOUR. Your husband and I are just discussing a
photograph. Or we will be, just as soon as he's found time in
his schedule for a brief glance.

DEBBIE. I'll make sure he does.

THE NEIGHBOUR. Would you mind, I'd be so grateful.
Before you two get started on one of your evenings. Five
minutes!

He withdraws.

DEBBIE. What photograph?

PETER. Christ knows, something to do with the garden.

DEBBIE. Where there's a policeman apparently.

ELSA *has come through the back door and now emerges from the kitchen in time to hear this.*

ELSA. Oh, don't you worry about the cop, honey. I'll take care of him.

DEBBIE. What's he doing here?

ELSA. Oh, they always show up, don't they, cops. With all their 'investigating'. Who gave them the right? That's what I want to know!

DEBBIE. What are they investigating?

ELSA. Oh, who cares? It's like an obsession with these people. Why do they have to find out things all time? What's wrong with a little mystery in our lives?

DEBBIE. No, but specifically what are they investigating?

ELSA. I gave him tea and sandwiches, he's still in the garden.

ELSA *is heading for the stairs.*

PETER. Does he want to talk to us?

ELSA. Maybe, I don't know. They just like asking questions, these guys, so they can write things down – it's very unhealthy.

DEBBIE. Well, what would he want to talk to us *about*?

PETER. Has something happened?

ELSA. Barnaby.

PETER. What about Barnaby?

ELSA. I told you about Barnaby, right?

PETER. He died.

ELSA. He's dead, yes.

PETER. So what's happened?

ELSA. He got worse.

PETER. ...sorry, worse?

ELSA. Much worse. Now he's been murdered.

PETER *and* DEBBIE *exchange a stressed glance.*

This is very tragic for me. I'm on a roller coaster.

PETER. Why do they want to talk to you?

ELSA. They can't help themselves. To them everything is an
'investigation'. Can't they leave murdered people in peace?
Haven't they suffered enough? Don't murdered people have
any right to privacy?

DEBBIE. But why – … why are they talking to *you*, Elsa?

ELSA. Oh, I guess, because I spent a week with him before
I got here.

DEBBIE. Sorry, what?

ELSA. Just a week of innocent companionship.

DEBBIE. But when you first got here, you said you'd come
straight from the airport.

ELSA. Did I?

DEBBIE. Yes, you did. You absolutely did. You said you'd just
flown in from Denver.

ELSA. How interesting!

DEBBIE. Now you're telling us you'd been in London for
a whole week before you even got here.

ELSA. Well, it's a grey area, isn't it? Let's agree on that. If you'll
excuse me, I have to go pack.

PETER. Are you leaving?

ELSA. Oh, I just like to pack every now and then, in case of
any events.

ELSA *now heading up the stairs.*

DEBBIE. Elsa… are you a suspect?

ELSA. Could you be a little more specific, dear?

DEBBIE. In Barnaby's murder.

ELSA. Oh, no, no. Just at the talking stage. You know men, they take ages before they get round to the subject. I made him sandwiches.

PETER. So you're *not* a suspect?

ELSA. Nobody's a suspect, sweetie, they think it's food poisoning.

DEBBIE. Food poisoning?

PETER. You just said it was murder.

ELSA. Tom*a*yto, tom*ah*to.

(*Heading up the stairs.*) If I have to leave suddenly could you say goodbye to the kids for me.

She heads up the stairs out of sight.

PETER *and* DEBBIE *look at each. Shit. Shit!!*

PC JUNKIN *has appeared through from the back garden. He's already deposited the milk back in the fridge, and teacup in the sink.*

He now appears through the living-room door with a large plate which has a single sandwich remaining on it.

PC JUNKIN. Can I use your toilet?

They stare at him for a moment. Thrown. Not sure what to say.

Sorry. Hello. Should have introduced myself earlier. PC Junkin, Dellside Station – I've just been talking to Elsa. Call me Phil, if you like. Or Dave. There were three Daves at the station already so I was moved on.

(*Still their stares.*) Can I use your toilet?

DEBBIE. What were you talking to Elsa about?

PC JUNKIN. Just routine. One of her friends has passed on, very suddenly – a purely routine conversation, that's all.

PETER. About what?

PC JUNKIN. Is it over there, the toilet? Would you mind?

He's pointing to the a toilet door, near the front door.

PETER. I'm sorry but we're going to need a bit more detail. Actually, a lot more detail, if you don't mind.

PC JUNKIN....Number twos.

PETER. No. No, I –

PC JUNKIN. Is that okay, downstairs? Some people are sensitive about solids near their living areas.

PETER. No, it's fine, we'd just like to know a bit more about what you were saying to Elsa.

PC JUNKIN....Would you mind if I went to the toilet first? Too many sandwiches!

DEBBIE *looks sharply at the plate.*

DEBBIE. Did Elsa make those?

PC JUNKIN. Yes, sorry. Couldn't stop her, she was like a machine. Every time I opened my mouth, she popped one in. It was like being a postbox at Christmas. Or a turkey. Excuse me!

DEBBIE. Are you... feeling okay?

PC JUNKIN. Yes, yes, just a bit –

(*Pats stomach.*) I could go upstairs, if you're concerned about... particles.

They shake their heads – No, it's fine. PC JUNKIN *disappears into the toilet.*

PETER *and* DEBBIE *look at each other.*

PETER. No, it's ridiculous. She wouldn't.

DEBBIE *grabs his arm, pulls him to the kitchen, safely out of* PC JUNKIN'*s earshot.*

DEBBIE. She wouldn't what? What wouldn't Elsa do? Kill people?

PETER. Not here, not in our house.

DEBBIE. Do you actually believe that?

PETER. She's been here for nearly a week, she hasn't killed anyone –

DEBBIE. For Christ's sake!

PETER. – we don't have to leap to conclusions, that's all I'm saying.

DEBBIE. Okay! How about this?

She grabs the sandwich plate with its solitary sandwich.

Would you eat this sandwich?

PETER....why?

DEBBIE. Would you eat it?

PETER....yeah.

DEBBIE. Would you though?

PETER. Yes.

DEBBIE. Would you *actually* eat it, for real? Would you eat it, in front of me, right now?

She's shoved it right under his nose. He's clearly uneasy.

PETER....within reason.

DEBBIE. What does that mean?

PETER. Maybe a corner.

DEBBIE. Why only a corner? What's the point in that? You either think she's a serial killer, or you don't. You either think that sandwich is poisoned or you don't. What's the point in only eating a corner?? What's your strategy?

She shoves the sandwich plate into his hands – he now clutches it throughout the next sequence.

PETER....splitting the difference.

DEBBIE. *Christ!!* We have let that woman into our house – she cooks for us, she hangs out with our kids – but we don't trust her enough to eat a sandwich she made for a policeman. *What's wrong with us?*

PETER. There's nothing wrong with us. We're just reasonable.

DEBBIE *storms over to one of the kitchen units, snatches up the laptop that's lying there.*

What are you doing?

DEBBIE. Panicking. I'm going online, it's what I do when I panic. Check he's all right.

PETER. Who?

DEBBIE. The policemen, Dave, Phil – check on him.

PETER *glances towards the toilet door.*

PETER. ... Well, he's barely started – it's probably a bit early to take a view –

DEBBIE. Go and check on him or phone an ambulance.

PETER. Why?

DEBBIE. What if he's dying?

PETER. What if he isn't?

DEBBIE. A policeman might be being murdered in our house *right now.* If he dies, what do we say? Yes, we did realise that our houseguest was a serial poisoner, but we couldn't think of a polite way to raise the subject before your officer shat himself to death in our downstairs loo. Phone an ambulance, just do it.

PETER. Okay, yes, understood, but just thinking of the bigger picture for one moment – if he doesn't die, won't it be really embarrassing that we phoned an ambulance?

DEBBIE. If he *does* die, won't it be really embarrassing that we *didn't* phone an ambulance?

PETER. It's very unfair that we've been put in this position.

DEBBIE. By *ourselves*.

PETER....I'll go and check on him.

DEBBIE. Her second husband –

PETER. Sorry, what?

DEBBIE. I'm on the website. Her second husband had blood in his bowel movements, that's how he knew what was going on. Same symptom as her first husband and her father...

PETER. Right –

DEBBIE. Ask him.

PETER. What?

DEBBIE. *Ask him!*

PETER. How??

DEBBIE. *Just do it!*

She propels him to the door.

Now they're both in the living room again. DEBBIE *urging* PETER *on.* PETER *hesitating towards the toilet door.*

Almost there, a despairing PETER *turns, looks pleadingly to* DEBBIE. *What the hell does he say??*

'Just do it!', signals DEBBIE.

PETER, *resigned, steps to the toilet door. (As he goes, he sets down the plate with the single sandwich on the table at the foot of the stairs.)*

PETER. Um. Hello? Dave? Or is it Phil?

PC JUNKIN (*from off*). Either is fine, sir. Everything all right?

PETER. Yes, yes, everything's all right out here.

Looks to DEBBIE. *'Just do it!' she signals.*

How's everything going on in there?

PC JUNKIN (*from off*). All fine, sir.

PETER. Good, good.

Looks to DEBBIE. *'Keep going' she signals.*

Is it all… you know… normal?

PC JUNKIN (*from off*). Normal?

PETER. So far?

PC JUNKIN (*from off*). What do you mean, normal?

PETER. No, no, I was just wondering… if you'd had a chance to… you know… have a quick look.

PC JUNKIN (*from off*). At what?

PETER. Just a little peek.

PC JUNKIN (*from off*). A peek at what, sir?

PETER.…below.

PC JUNKIN (*from off*). Below?

PETER. Below… basically… you.

A terrible silence. PETER *and* DEBBIE *looking at each other. Christ! Oh, Christ!!*

PC JUNKIN (*from off*). Not really, sir, no.

PETER.…are you planning to?

PC JUNKIN (*from off*). I wasn't, in fact.

PETER.…okay. Okay, that's fine. No problem. Your choice.

A pause as he flails for a way to continue.

Can I?

Silence as PETER *cringes, and* DEBBIE *despairs.*

I'll be quick.

PC JUNKIN (*from off*).….I'm sorry, sir, I don't think I'm quite understanding…

PETER. It's nothing, nothing, sorry, no! What I'm trying to ask is – basically – if you were to… glance… downwards… is

there… you know, among all the normal… elements… are
there any traces of… oh, I don't know… blood, or anything?

PC JUNKIN (*from off*). Blood, sir?

PETER. It's nothing, don't be alarmed, ignore me. It's just…
we've had a lot of problems with that toilet, and I wanted to
make sure it wasn't playing up again.

PC JUNKIN (*from off*). What do you mean, playing up? What
sort of problems?

PETER. Nothing. Nothing at all, forget I even said that.

He looks to DEBBIE. *What the hell does he do now?*

DEBBIE *implores him.*

PC JUNKIN (*from off*). I'm just coming out now anyway, sir.

PETER. *Don't flush it!!*

PC JUNKIN (*from off*).…I'm sorry, sir?

PETER. Sorry. Sorry. No, I just – … I'll flush it for you.

PC JUNKIN (*from off*). Why, sir?

PETER. Well…

(*Flails desperately for something useful to say.*) You're a
busy man.

PC JUNKIN (*from off*). Sir?

PETER. It's just that toilet. I mean it's fine, it's just a bit… on
the edge.

The toilet door opens. A bemused PC JUNKIN *steps from
within it. Staring, puzzled, at* PETER.

Thank you. Thank you. So much.

PC JUNKIN (*embarrassed*). I, ah… put the lid down, obviously.

He gestures. PETER *goes quickly into the toilet. It's a very
small room, so he's still visible within it, even if the toilet
itself isn't.*

PETER *looking down at the out-of-sight toilet.*

PETER. Oh, yes. So you did. Look at that.

PC JUNKIN. Spare you the full horror of my lunch!

He shoots a sheepish look at DEBBIE, *who forces a quick smile back at him.*

PETER *is still looking down at the toilet. Damn!*

PETER. Yes, of course, very thoughtful. Thank you.

(*Takes a breath. Braces himself.*) But you know what? Long as I'm here, I might as well… you know, just have a little… peek.

As PC JUNKIN *stares in astonishment,* PETER *has bent over out of sight. We hear the squeak of the raising lid.*

Ah, yes. Very good. Good-oh. Well, that all seems to be in order. All good so far, yes. I mean there was a lot of paper, I couldn't really see…

DEBBIE *despairs at him. They need to do this.*

PETER *resolves himself. He now grabs the lavatory brush.*

Might as well be… you know… thorough.

He bends to poke around in the toilet.

ROSIE *is coming down the stairs – sees* PC JUNKIN.

ROSIE. What's going on?

DEBBIE. Nothing, nothing –

PETER *pops out of the toilet, toilet brush still in hand.*

PETER. Oh, Rosie. There you are.

ROSIE. What are you doing?

PETER. Oh, you know –

There are no first-class explanations.

This is PC Junkin. Call him Dave. Or Phil.

PC JUNKIN. I was just using the toilet.

PETER. Yes, he was just using the toilet, and I've been…
helping.

ROSIE. *Helping??*

PETER. It's a difficult toilet, as you know.

ROSIE. No, it isn't.

PETER. Yes, it is, Rosie! Don't lie to the police!

ROSIE. How is it difficult?

PETER. It's… edgy.

And now ALEX *comes bursting back in* (*leaving the door open*).

ALEX. Sorry, sorry, fart coming.

PETER. Well, don't bring it in here.

ALEX (*heading to the toilet*). There were people out there –
you said go to the toilet. I'm doing what you *said*.

He has pushed his way past PETER, *gone into the toilet.
Now recoils in horror.*

Oh my God, what's that?

PETER. That wasn't me, it was the policeman.

PC JUNKIN. He said he wanted a look.

PETER. I wasn't *looking*, I was *helping*. You know we have
a lot of difficulty with that toilet.

ALEX. No, we don't!

PETER. Yes, we do, it's edgy. It's an edgy toilet.

ALEX. What are you talking about?

PETER. Look. The toilet is edgy, the policeman's stools are
perfectly healthy, and the sandwiches are not poisoned Are
we all clear on that?? Everybody clear?

Dumb nodding all round.

Good! Excellent! Well done, team!

He rounds on PC JUNKIN.

Dave. Phil. It's been a pleasure. Thanks for stopping by.
Sorry to hear about Elsa's friend, I'm sure you'll get the
whole thing cleared up. I've said it before, and I'll say it
again – our policemen are wonderful! Is that everything?
Great! Bye!

Behind him, THE NEIGHBOUR *has appeared through the
door, now is standing at* PETER*'s shoulder.*

THE NEIGHBOUR. Photo?

PETER *finally breaks. A huge outburst.*

PETER. Oh for *fuck's sake, for fuck's sake, for fuck's sake.
Would everybody just leave me alone!!*

*He turns and just storms into the toilet, slams the door – just
as* ELSA *comes down the stairs.*

ELSA (*to* THE NEIGHBOUR). Oh, it's my handsome tea
partner. I had a look at the photograph you sent. I'm afraid
that wall is clearly yours and any repair costs are on you.

THE NEIGHBOUR (*a good-natured laugh*). Yes, I thought that
was probably the case, but one has to try.

ELSA. No hard feelings, I'm sure.

THE NEIGHBOUR. None at all.

ELSA (*noticing the sandwich plate*). Oh, there's one left.

*She picks up the sandwich and, happily munching on it,
heads into the kitchen.*

Leaving everyone just staring at one another.

PC JUNKIN *nods towards the toilet door.*

PC JUNKIN. Is he all right?

THE NEIGHBOUR. He's a busy man.

As the lights fade we hear the toilet flush.

Peter and Debbie's House

The lights come up on –

The house in silence again.

Once again, THE NEIGHBOUR *is sitting, motionless, and silent. This time he's sitting at the kitchen table, a cup of tea in front of him. He is staring straight ahead, his usual patience. He takes a sip of tea.*

Stillness. Silence.

Then a car horn hoots outside.

PETER *comes clattering down the stairs, carrying one of* ELSA*'s bags.*

He puts the bag by the front door, opens it and calls out:

PETER. She'll be right out.

> *He leaves the door open as* ALEX *and* ROSIE *are coming down the stairs, also carrying some of* ELSA*'s bags.*

ROSIE. This is sad. I hate this.

ALEX. She can't stay forever, Rosie.

ROSIE (*to* PETER). Will she ever be coming back?

PETER. She's… fairly hard to predict.

> DEBBIE *is coming down the stairs.*

DEBBIE. Seriously? Is this the goodbye committee?

ALEX. You coming to join it?

DEBBIE. On the understanding that, should I ever leave this house, for however short a time, I get this level of fuss.

ALEX. Nah.

ROSIE. Because we love you too much to ever let you go.

> *And she gives her mother a huge hug.*

> PETER *and* DEBBIE *look at each other – incomprehension. What the fuck?!*

And now ELSA *is descending the stairs, as grandly as she can.*

ELSA. Look at this family. Oh my God, *look at this family*! I could mash you all up in a giant bowl and roll around in you. Look at you!!

ROSIE. I've discussed it with my brother. We're against you leaving.

ELSA. Elsa Jean Krakowski knows when her work is done.

PETER. Your car is here.

ELSA. Thank you, Peter. Oh, I'm gonna miss this man!

DEBBIE. Have a safe flight.

ELSA. Safe? Who wants a safe flight, gimme bumpy. I might meet someone! Now, Rosie, listen, girl! Your parents. They're the best. You never forget that, right. Gonna miss you, clever little Rosie. And Alex – computer games are not exercise, you got me? They're awesome, but they're not exercise. See you online sometime – we got Mexican Polacks to kill.

ALEX. Yep. Let's kill Mexican Polacks. Or anyone, really.

ELSA. You're talking my language, babe.

(*To* PETER.) Peter. One day, and it won't be long, you're going to start missing your mom for the rest of your life. Nothing can change that. But you can change all the days between now and then – do you hear me?

PETER. Well. Yes.

ELSA. When people are gone, they're gone. Take it from Elsa.

(*Turns to* DEBBIE.) Debbie. Been a pleasure!

DEBBIE *waits expectantly. There's nothing more.*

DEBBIE....is that it? Is that all I get?

ELSA. Oh, and Peter. Your neighbour. He's a pain in the ass. You need to know that. The cups of tea I've made for that

man, and it's all the passive-aggressive, all of the time.
Someone should drop a plane on that guy.

DEBBIE. So we're back on Peter now.

ELSA (*to both of them*). Oh, you two. You know who you
remind me of? Me and my first husband.

PETER. Right. Well, good.

DEBBIE (*nervously jocular*). Well, I hope we're not *too* similar.

ELSA. No, you are, very, very similar.

DEBBIE. Well, I hope not *completely* similar.

ELSA. Why would you say that?

DEBBIE. Well – you know. You murdered him.

*And that sentence lands like a bomb. A dreadful, ringing
silence.*

PETER (*reproving*). Debbie!

DEBBIE.…what? *What??* I wasn't supposed to mention that?

ROSIE. Mum!

DEBBIE. Look it up online. Go on, do it. It's true.

ALEX. Mum – you can't believe everything you read online.

DEBBIE. She murdered her first husband. She did. And now,
she's comparing your father and me, to her and the man she
murdered.

ELSA. Debbie Lindel, I'm surprised at you. Do you really think
it's possible to judge twenty years of marriage on one
murder?

Another silence.

PETER. Well – if one of you murdered the other, yes, kind of.

ELSA. Oh for God's sake. I mean, jeez. Look into your hearts.
In a very real, human sense, haven't we all, at some point,
murdered a few people?

PETER.…No.

ELSA. Oh. Just me then.

> (*Roars with laughter.*) Look at you all! Look at your little
> faces! I'm not a murderer! Of course I'm not. I don't *enjoy*
> killing people. It's not a hobby. Now and then, I just have
> a very strong feeling that it would be better if certain people
> were dead – and I don't think it's healthy to keep feelings
> like that bottled up. I'm a *doing* person. Is it a crime to be
> a doing person?

DEBBIE. Yes. If what you're doing is murdering people.

ELSA. Why? I mean honestly, think about it, why? What's so
  terribly wrong about murdering a few carefully selected
  people now and then? Do you really think the human race is
  unimprovable? My old dad said to me – just before he died –
  'Elsa, try and make the whole world a better place one
  human being at time.' I started that very day, and God
  willing, I'm never going to stop.

> *Horrified silence. And* ELSA *roars with laughter again.*

> Oh, Debbie, your little face. I could peel it right off and
> stitch it on a throw pillow. Do I *seem* like a murderer? Do
> I *act* like a murderer?

DEBBIE. No, but… well…

ELSA. No, but you read it somewhere. No, but if it says so
  online it must be true. Debbie, wake up. You know me.
  You've met me. Never mind the facts, what's your lived
  experience? What have you seen, what have you felt? Does
  nothing you see and hear for yourself matter, if the facts say
  different? Honey. Listen to me. What's right in front of you
  might not be the whole truth, it might not be the truth you
  were looking for, but I'll tell you something… it's *your* truth.

> DEBBIE, *lost now, unsure.*

DEBBIE. But did you… Are you…

> ELSA *places a finger on* DEBBIE*'s lips, silencing her.*

ELSA. One day everybody will know everything there is to know. And on that day everything will be over. Who wants that?

DEBBIE, *properly stumped now – and now* PC JUNKIN *appears through the door and starts picking up* ELSA*'s bags.*

PC JUNKIN. Is this everything, Elsa?

ELSA. That's lovely, thank you. I'll be right with you.

PETER....Dave?

PC JUNKIN. Hello, sir. How's the toilet?

PETER. Oh, it's... you know... settling down.

PC JUNKIN *disappears off, carrying all the bags.*

ELSA. Dave kindly agreed to give me a ride to the airport because of all your urban violence.

DEBBIE. You have a police escort??

ELSA. It's the times we live in, Debbie. A person could get murdered.

(*Heading to the door.*) Now, listen to me, lovely Lindels. Goodbye is the worst word in the world. When I look back, I don't want my last memory of people I love to be them saying goodbye. So you all just stand there, and do nothing. Plain nothing. Just look adorable and British, like you're waiting in line, and that'll do Elsa just fine.

PC JUNKIN *now reappears as if wondering where* ELSA*'s got to. She doesn't even look round, just hands him her handbag.*

You forgot this one.

PC JUNKIN. Oh, sorry.

He hurries off, taking her handbag. ELSA *looks round the Lindels – her final goodbye.*

ELSA. Oh, look at you. My little Lindels. Bless you all.

(Moves to the door.) Elsa Jean Krakowski…

(Steps over the threshold.) …has left the building.

With flourish, she slams the door.

A moment's silence.

They all look at each other.

ALEX. What was all that about? Elsa murdering people?

PETER. God knows. God honestly knows. Cup of tea?

DEBBIE. Could I have tea with wine in it, but no actual tea and just wine?

PETER. Special Mummy tea for you, just tea for you two. Okay?

ROSIE. Fine.

ALEX. Yeah, why not?

ROSIE. Family night in. Awesome.

PETER *smiles, happy at that thought.*

He heads through to the kitchen –

– and freezes in horror. Because the poor old NEIGHBOUR *is still sitting there.*

PETER. Oh, Christ, sorry, sorry, got distracted. How do I keep doing that?? The hedge-trimming rota, yeah? I'm four-and-a-half years behind – sounds about right. I'll have a look at that email right now. If I can find it.

(Starts scrolling through his phone.) That was Elsa leaving, by the way. Can't quite believe I'm saying this, but I'm going to miss her. I mean, strange woman… and dear God, please never, ever google her… but she made a difference, didn't she? Livened the place up. Which is sort of the opposite of what I was expecting, to be honest. Anyway – brace yourself, you'll have to start making your own tea now.

He registers that THE NEIGHBOUR *isn't replying in any way. Frowns. Touches* THE NEIGHBOUR*'s shoulder.*

And THE NEIGHBOUR *pitches forward and slams face-down on the table, clearly stone dead.*

Curtain.

The End.

www.nickhernbooks.co.uk

facebook.com/nickhernbooks

twitter.com/nickhernbooks